Dear Mr Leac

Dear Mr Leach

SOME THOUGHTS ON CERAMICS

Sebastian Blackie

A & C Black
London

First published in Great Britain in 2004
A & C Black Publishers Limited
Alderman House, 37 Soho Square
London W1D 3QZ
www.acblack.com

ISBN 0-7136-6942-X

CIP Catalogue records for this book are available from the British Library and the U.S. Library of Congress.

Book design by Susan McIntyre
Cover design by Dorothy Moir
Copyedited and proofread by Michelle Fisher

Printed and bound in Singapore by Tien Wah Press

A & C Black uses paper produced with elemental chlorine-free pulp, harvested from managed sustainable forests.

Front cover photograph: Peter Kinnear
Back cover photograph: Sebastian Blackie
Frontispiece: Jar, coiled and wire cut by the author
Below and opposite: Ceramic 'hangups' by the author
Title page: Bowl with one foot by the author

Contents

Acknowledgements 7

Introduction 9

Words on Paper 12

Firing the Imagination 14

Umbilical Cord 16

Empty Vessels 18

Beggars and Choosers 21

Slaves 24

Free, Forty, Five, Sex
  and Seven 26

No Ware 28

Making Sense 30

Basket Case 32

Relative Values 34

Boredom 36

Gifts 38

Hard Ground 40

Learner 42

Fact and Fiction 44

Weaving Facts 46

Earth, Air, Fire and Water 50

Good Deal 53

Pen to Paper 56

Going Back 60

Sun and Moon 62

Through a Glass Darkly 64

High Street Glaze 66

Handles 70

Pit 72

Slip of a Thing 74

Tools 76

Lips 78

Weight and See 80

Yalc! 82

Atoms 84

Humanity and Inhumanity 87

Rules 90

Silent Channel 92

Translation 94

The Garden of Eden 96

Kiss 98

Banali 100

Big Idea 102

Joining Hands 104

Remember 106

Bill 108

Ceramic Heaven 110

Death on the Nile 113

Nest 115

No-thing 118

Begin-again 120

Biographies 123

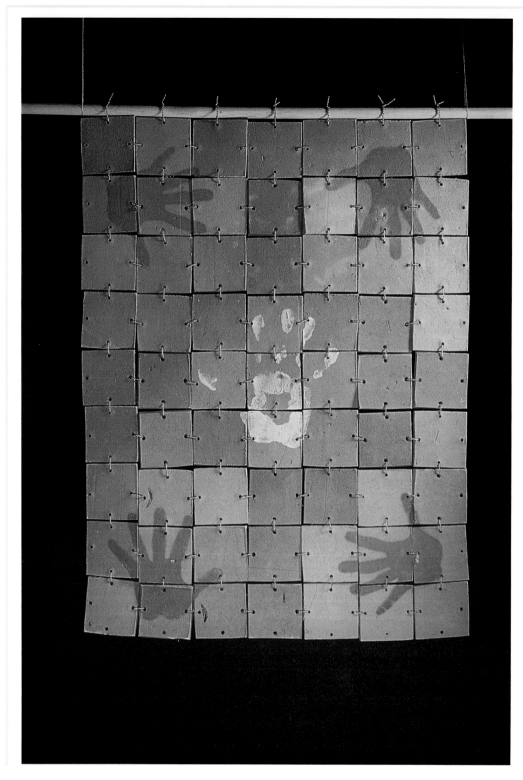

Tile panel

Acknowledgements

Writing, like making, can be solitary. In my case it has been, in part, collaborative. This book would not have been conceived, let alone published, without the help of many people. I thank the numerous enthusiasts, too many to name, who have helped me make kilns from paper – their faith and commitment in such an unlikely enterprise has been essential. I dedicate this book to them.

It is difficult to communicate how important it has been for me to visit Japan as Rioji Koie's guest, because I do not really understand it myself. The form of this book came from writing to my wife Sarah each day I was there. Deprived of spoken communication (and much else), which normally gives an allusion of power, I re-learnt to listen, look and think.

Kate Weitheim and Merran Esson made a special contribution. Our informal discussions, over excellent Dove Café coffee under the intense Australian sun, helped me to focus on the possibility of a book that went beyond technical description.

I am deeply grateful to Anita Besson of Galerie Besson. Her enthusiasm for my strangely spelt drafts has been immensely encouraging, and by offering to undertake the arduous task of proofreading the writings of a dyslexic she has extended her gallery work of bringing artists and public together.

I am indebted to the polymath Professor James Crabb, fellow of Wolfson College Oxford, and Professor Tony Franks, potter, one time principal of Edinburgh College of Art, and currently president of the International Ceramics Academy, for their incisive criticism. I not only value their suggestions but also take some humble pleasure in the skill and precision with which the flaws in my writing have been identified.

There are many others: tinsmith Mathew Harding and basket weaver Polly Pollark, generous spirits, willing to both share and risk their specialist knowledge. I am grateful for their curiosity and playfulness. I hope through

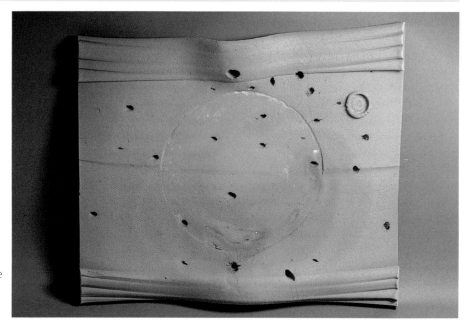

Wire-cut dish made from Sussex brick clay by the author

our contact they feel able to promote practice, which practically celebrates the extraordinary and the ridiculous.

A very special thanks to my friend Margaret O'Rorke, fellow potter and dreamer of building castles in the air from real bricks. Our long discussions, often till dawn, over many years (and bottles of wine) have given me the confidence to believe in the legitimacy of the ideas expressed in this book.

I apologise to my children, Thea and Lucie, who have been pressed into assisting in my pyrotechnic schemes, but I think we had some fun in the process. I owe my greatest debt to Sarah, whose faith in me, or the project, (I am not sure which) has been a major support. Since our marriage I have been somewhat absent, either overseas or up the garden in my studio. Sarah knows that a statement such as 'I am just checking something in the studio/on the computer' is usually followed by many hours, or months, of absence. She has patiently listened to draft texts on my return; her thoughtful comments often prompting my further protracted disappearance. In a few weeks we expect our first baby together. If Elizabeth, my third, amazing daughter, is to know her father, it seems this book has been completed just in time.

June 2003

Introduction

Apparently, the fictional detective Hercule Poirot saved my life. My mother was convinced that my eccentric behaviour was due to brain damage at birth, but that it would have been even worse if she had not refused the anaesthetic in order to continue reading her book to find out 'who-dunnit'. I do seem to have spent my life gathering seemingly random clues that might explain what I am doing here. Perhaps, as a dyslexic, what few little grey cells I have are drawn to learning by making – accessing the mysteries of life through practice rather than theory. Perhaps I have found a particular affinity with clay because it has no form in itself; the clues are not intrinsic but emerge through work. A clouded mirror reflecting the inner man.

This book is a series of e-mails to Bernard Leach. The deceased father, some would say godfather, of the modern studio ceramic movement. By contextualising craft with a philosophy, he inspired people all over the world to value hand work. He introduced to the West a way of looking at pots that he had learnt in Japan, and coined the term 'head, hand and heart' to express a sense of equilibrium which he believed industrial societies needed to regain. In 1940 he published *A Potter's Book* in which he provided both advice on traditional making methods and a modernist's view on beauty.

Dear Mr Leach similarly combines practical information with philosophy but of a very different kind. It examines the technology of so-called primitive cultures and finds equivalents in 'developed' urban environments. It describes how to make kilns with paper and glazes with toothpaste. It challenges Leach's ideas in the context of such issues as memory, gender, sustainability and spirituality while at the same time acknowledging the debt that all craftspeople owe him by his insistence that their work is serious. It explores how we learn and questions why and what we make. It gives a personal reflection on my visits to Japan, Korea, India and Australia, exploring the nature of cultural exchange and unfolds like a diary of my life and practice over the many months it has taken to write.

'Ceramic carpet'
made from
saggar-fired tiles
by the author

The Sudanese potter Siddig El Nigoumi told me his first experience of clay was as a child on the banks of the Nile because 'there was nothing else to play with'. There are many children today, their imaginations suffocated by a flood of mass-produced toys, who might be envious if they knew the elemental delights of clay and fire. I hope *Dear Mr Leach* is of value to makers but may also appeal to those who find it difficult to understand our obsession with clay; stimulating the creative impulse we all seem to be born with and bringing a new understanding of this extraordinary material.

'Urn' made from saggar-fired stoneware, by the author

To: Bernard Leach <bleach@ceramicheaven.com>
From: Sebastian Blackie <black@restlessearth.co.uk>

Subject: *Words on Paper*

Dear Mr Leach

Thank you for your letter of the 19th October 1966. I am sorry to have taken so long to reply. Being dyslexic has not helped me to be a good correspondent but has been a wonderful advantage as a potter. It encouraged me to learn empirically, to observe and to play. Because I am used to 'getting things wrong' I am also used to 'trying things out' even when, to most people, they may seem ridiculous. Pottery saved me at school. It was the first thing that I was good at and began to give me some self esteem. Ceramics helped me to learn something about maths, physics and chemistry, anthropology and geology. I needed them to progress with the clay and could understand them through the clay. Ceramics, which you did so much to introduce to schools in the 1950s, is now fast disappearing from the curriculum.

The teacher who asked me when I was eight whether I was lazy or stupid will be surprised that I am attempting to write a book. Although it contains practical information, I hope the readers will understand that it is as much about firing the imagination as firing clay. I hope the readers will not take the text as 'the only way to do it' but a tool to explore the world with. In the developed world most of us now live in towns and cities. When you and Hamada started the workshop in St Ives you travelled around rural Cornwall to find your raw materials. I remember when I first read *A Potter's Book* I felt you were writing as much about what being a potter was, as about how to make pots. That making one's own tools and kilns, and digging the clay, developed an intimacy with material and process that liberated work from the conformity of industrialisation.

Although I love to pot, I am beginning to question whether the world really needs any more stuff. We are weighed down by objects. I think there is some future in using my ceramic knowledge to make fire sculptures; the performances seem to provoke creativity, as well as wonder, in the audience.

When you first started to pot at the beginning of the 20th century, your ideas on the importance of balance between head, hand and heart must have been radical. Given urgency due to the industrialised killings of World War I. Today the computer, and much else, has, I think, prioritised that part of the brain we use for rational thought and further eroded the individual ability to develop as multi-sensual beings. Most of us have become dependent consumers with little understanding of how things work or are made.

Best wishes
Sebastian Blackie

Letter from Bernard Leach
to Sebastian Blackie

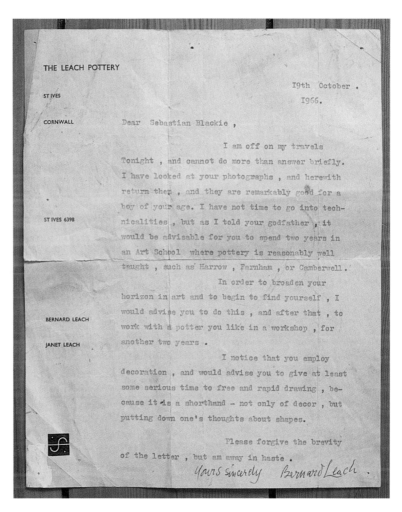

To: Bernard Leach <bleach@ceramicheaven.com>
From: Sebastian Blackie <black@restlessearth.co.uk>

Subject: *Firing the Imagination*

Dear Mr Leach

Japan was extraordinary. When I remember my time there it is more like a dream than a memory.

Japan offers a completely different way of thinking about ceramics; not just in products and process but also its place within society. The Japanese seem to 'read' pots at a much more sophisticated level than in the West. We visited a ceramic school near Toyota where the students (all part-time 'hobby' potters) were firing a great Anagama kiln. Wood fired, a single chamber about 15m (50ft) long and big enough to stand up in. All the classes were taking it in turns to stoke the kiln for the five days of the firing. In the West, wood kilns are associated with a macho, independent and alternative approach to society – a tool of individuality. I felt in Japan that these kilns, and presumably their products, expressed community and collaboration.

Western rationalism seems to have produced a culture of measurement and control. For example, we struggle to make our kilns fire evenly throughout. With the Anagama, the Japanese adjust their work to fit the particular conditions of each part of the kiln as a gardener might choose plants for different places in the garden.

In the Ohara Museum of Art I saw an exhibition of your work together with that of Hamada. For the first time I felt its English spirit but also an excitement I have not identified in the work you made in England. The museum also had a collection of Jasper Johns and Jackson Pollock. Suddenly I understood how you and Hamada are seen as modernist innovators in Japan. The avant-garde in Britain seems to ignore history except in a limited, post-modern, literary sense; in Japan the avant-garde seems more cutting-edge precisely because it is informed by the past.

Many felt your emphasis on tradition was stifling. Do you think this may be something to do with ceramic 'illiteracy' where style is confused with content, techniques associated with particular ideologies?

I discovered that Oribe ware, for me very exciting and quintessentially Japanese, was considered to come from Europe. I began to wonder whether we tend to only recognise and value that which we are already familiar with and need help if we are to expand our experience. Perhaps that is why I feel the paper kilns are so important. They oblige us to think differently, a kind of ceramic therapy that allows us to approach things in a new way, extending our values and developing our tastes.

The food in Japan was very unfamiliar to me but nevertheless a multi-sensual feast. Food and pots produce wonderful visual and tactile relationships. When I first arrived I suddenly realised that chopsticks allow for much more diverse ceramic surfaces than knives and forks. Tools, like language, have a direct influence on the trajectory of our imagination.

Best wishes
Sebastian Blackie

*Hamada's house,
Mashiko, Japan*

To: Bernard Leach <bleach@ceramicheaven.com>
From: Sebastian Blackie <black@restlessearth.co.uk>

Subject: *Umbilical Cord*

Dear Mr Leach

I remember making my first pots as a child from clay, dug with my hands, from the bed of the brook that ran through our village. Nobody taught me, except perhaps the clay itself. I can still recall its cool, wet slipperiness, its smell, and its colour, which changed from gray to tan as it dried and oxidised. In Japan I used clay dug from the mountain, some almost black, full of great lumps of charred wood, perhaps the result of volcanic action. Another was bright orange and very low in plasticity; I think iron oxide with a bit of clay. I

Mashiko, Japan

mixed this with clay from Shigaraki which, when fired, gave a deep, mahogany brown. Each time the clay was different and without a test kiln I had to rely on instinct or at least, as if pregnant, accept what was delivered.

Working in Japan was like finding ceramics for the first time. Stripped of much that gave an illusion of security at home, I had to relearn to trust in a way that children do naturally. For 40 days in Japan I explored my own wilderness – often lost but always excited. I resisted the temptation of making things I knew I could make. Effectively deprived of speech, I learnt to question myself more and others less. I became more economical in my movements, my use of space and materials. I learnt not to burden myself with information before I needed it and began to question the value of so much that I had already acquired. In so doing I found a calm in the face of failure. We may be encouraged by success but it might be more encouraging to recognise that success is not necessarily the best teacher.

I remember Lucie Rie telling a student 'without skill you are never free'. As we grow into adulthood we need to develop skill like a vocabulary to successfully express ever more complex ideas; but succinctness is a talent. In Japan I disciplined myself to use the minimum skill. I looked for the minimum means to achieve my intention. I learnt to listen.

The development of my paper kilns has depended on this listening or observing approach but I know I have also been supported by technical theory. Sometimes, however, this knowledge has blinded me and I know that listening to the often technically naïve, but imaginative, questions of others has helped. What then should we teach? What should I include in this book which provides others with the information they need but also gives the reader space? In *Beyond East and West* you quote Blake, 'What is now proved was once only imagined'.

I never saw Koie (Ryoji Koie, one of Japan's most important contemporary ceramic artists) teaching the assistants in the way we in the West tend to teach. They worked extraordinarily hard on the most menial of tasks yet he would wake them without mercy at any hour if he wanted help. He expected, and got, total dedication. I remember the emotional last night before So (Koie's assistant) left for Korea having worked with Koie for many months. We stayed up all night drinking. Koie lectured So, who never lost eye contact, in a monologue that lasted for hours. At 4am Koie presented So with an ancient Korean pot made to hold an umbilical cord.

Best wishes
Sebastian Blackie

So making Korean-style pot

To: Bernard Leach <bleach@ceramicheaven.com>
From: Sebastian Blackie <black@restlessearth.co.uk>

Subject: *Empty Vessels*

▶ Attachment: Saké, Whiskey, Schnapps Cups

Dear Mr Leach

Since returning from Japan I have been inspired to work with unprocessed clay – clay as dug. I have been given four tons of wonderful Derbyshire fire clay. I don't think my reasons are nostalgic, but rather because each type of clay has a specific character which must be addressed. Dug clays are not uniform, so that each piece made is the result of negotiation between maker and material (like the tough kids I taught in London, these clays will not just accept what they are told to do). I feel the processed bodies offered by

The author at his computer

ceramic suppliers are by comparison bland and compliant. Materials, like metals, are worked after they have already been given man-made form: sheet, bar, tube etc. Working with plastic clay is a completely different way of thinking, as we start with a lumped mass; nevertheless the dug clays are not totally formless and, like the London kids, their individual nature must be respected and they need encouragement to sparkle.

I find writing this book interesting, as it requires two very different ways of working. I am stimulated by the precision needed to describe how things are made and look at application forms for visas or car tax with new interest; analysing how language has been simplified to be descriptive, unambiguous and accessible. My other messages to you are quite different. They are more speculative, three-dimensional. I am, as it were, thinking aloud. The use of words needs to be just as precise but in a resonant, poetic way if it is to be of any value to others.

As I write I become increasingly aware that the quality of this medium is very different from clay but also that the tools, pen or computer, influence thought just as throwing is a different way of thinking from slabbing. I am beginning to enjoy words for their texture, rhythm and shape in the same way I enjoy the visceral qualities of clay. In Japan I saw an exhibition of poetry that I could not read but in which I could find meaning nonetheless. Beautiful calligraphy, dark emphatic strokes or the brush running out of ink before the character is completed just as one might run out of breath when speaking. My great grandfather's diaries are difficult to decipher. Written with a quill pen, their power is 'read' as much from their physical, visual form, as from their literary meaning.

In this e-mail I had intended to discuss writing about ceramics but it has turned out to be just about writing. I enclose an attachment: a piece of text intended to inform the consumer by offering a few clues as to the motives behind the work. The work, a thousand cups, was held in the glass case of a museum, the proportion of a *tatami* mat, for over a year. The audience was invited to purchase a piece, freeing it from the museum world of glass cases, to become a living object through which memory work might be mediated.

Best wishes
Sebastian Blackie

▶ *Saké, Whiskey, Schnapps Cups*

These cups are some of over a thousand installed in a glass tank for the exhibition 'Cultural Exchange', part of the festival, 'Japan 2002', at Birmingham's City Art Gallery. It symbolises individual existence within mass culture and is about the intractability of dealing with the unimaginable; the desire to forget and the difficulty of remembering.

'Saké, Whiskey, Schnapps Cups'; installation with 1000 pots (detail) by the author

My work in this exhibition attempted to make sense of the unfamiliar, where, stripped of much that normally provides an illusion of security, and denied verbal communication, the mundane can become extraordinary. For me, in Japan, the rhythm of the spoken and written word gained value over literary meaning and objects acquired a kind of democracy; tea bowls and urinals were equally interesting. I used the rituals of drink, gestures of friendship and commemoration common to many cultures, but reflected on the irony of finding a terrible beauty in the domestic artifacts, individual possessions transformed by the atomic bomb, in Hiroshima's peace museum.

Two months later I visited the Jewish Museum in Sydney, Australia. The familiar grainy photographs of the Holocaust seemed oddly meaningless in a blatantly hedonistic city on the edge of such an ancient and a-European continent. The guides, all survivors, whose living testimony would soon be silenced, hourly recalling their shattered childhood memories to the few who would listen, was much more shocking.

'Saké, Whiskey, Schnapps Cups' by the author

To: Bernard Leach <bleach@ceramicheaven.com>
From: Sebastian Blackie <black@restlessearth.co.uk>

Subject: ***Beggars and Choosers***

Dear Mr Leach

I have just returned from two weeks in Delhi helping to mount an exhibition called 'Message to India' for the British Council. The work is by emerging British fine artists of Asian origin. Several overtly deal with issues of identity and their experience as British Indians. Three of the artists came to Delhi for the show and were exhilarated to be fêted by the press as independent young Asian women, but clearly struggled to deal with the many conflicting emotions that one is confronted with in India. Perhaps they recognised their 'Britishness' in a way they could not at home. The form of their work is contemporary Western, very different from the romantic and mystical work that we saw in the Delhi College of Art and artists' collective.

The Council is interested in a similar exhibition in the crafts (ceramics and textiles). This raises a number of questions: in craft is cultural fusion an issue or just a fact? Sarah, my wife, feels that UK children of Asian origin, at school level, retain their cultures' colour-sense and affinity with pattern. What message might such a group usefully send to India where a strong skill base of traditional craft still exists? The 'message' show was stimulating as an exhibition of young artists – bright, witty, irreverent, diverse and informed. The cultural element, however, gave it an extra dimension – the artists had confidently and consciously taken from both birthrights. They seem, without angst, to own but not to belong to both cultures. In their personal lives they may struggle with conflicting expectations of family and mainstream British society, but artistically they choose (but are also obliged) to construct a personal identity as pioneers of cultural fusion.

I expect you would feel that India has more to offer us than the other way round. In rural India, pots for everyday use and religious clay sculpture remain at the centre of the community, but one can see in the shopping emporia of Delhi that the crafts have been reduced to tourist tat. The skills remain but the work has lost its meaning; a sense of belonging to its culture. The Museum of Indian Terracotta at Sanskriti shows what is being lost but I cannot believe that this is something Westerners can reclaim. Preserve and interpret yes, acknowledge and value where it still remains vital, yes. The 'message' work was authentic but different because it springs from, and reflects, a different culture. Knowingness has replaced faith; having chosen we cannot go back.

Significant quantities of contemporary Western crafts show an attraction to techniques (and styles) associated with pre-industrial societies. They seem to give value to our common humanity; they speak of individual and personal relationships. Express the particular rather than the general. I warm to this work and its aspirations; it seems an alternative to so much offered by the developed world, but after facing the beggars of Delhi I am forced to think and feel again.

Best wishes
Sebastian Blackie

Potter, New Delhi.
PHOTO BY JANE
PERRYMAN, AUTHOR OF
'TRADITIONAL POTTERY
OF INDIA'
(2000, A&C BLACK)

To: Bernard Leach <bleach@ceramicheaven.com>
From: Sebastian Blackie <black@restlessearth.co.uk>

Subject: *Slaves*

Dear Mr Leach

To fly to Nagoya I had an eight hour stop-over at Singapore airport. I waited, jet lagged, in the humid cactus garden on the roof; smoking and drinking wine in a strange, tropical no-man's-land. It felt as if every nation in the world was united by nicotine addiction. I got talking to a German couple, both nurses, who had been travelling in Burma. She was from former East Germany, he from the West. They said they had seen shackled prisoners working on the roads and were reflective about themselves as tourists visiting a country so poor and repressed. We discovered our families had been travellers. He told me his grandfather had been a doctor in China in the 1930s and added, to my surprise, 'so he was not a Nazi'.

I have inherited my great grandfather's diaries. He was an intrepid traveller and in 1853 sailed to America arriving at the Mississippi delta and leaving over a year later from the St Lawrence. Amongst many adventures, he made a protest in a slave market in St Louis and before returning home visited his cousins in Bermuda, a British colony and thus by this time free of slavery, if not inequality. His great grandfather had led the Stewarts of Appin in all the key battles against the English in the Jacobite rebellion. Widowed, his wife, nine months pregnant, was expelled into the Scottish winter. She eventually settled in Paris. One son was my ancestor, another emigrated to Bermuda and became the governor.

It is interesting how family legends develop. How certain characteristics are selected and are passed on down the generations as something to aspire to. In some ways this seems a good thing – taking the best and passing it on – but equally it can breed a conditioned response which may not necessarily be the best strategy in a particular situation. Bruno Bettelheim identifies in his book *The Informed Heart* how annihilation in the extremes of the concentration camps was predictable for those who would not adjust to the new reality. Tradition offered no defence.

You made powerful arguments for working with a sense of tradition and ignited ideas that attracted many to handmade pottery in the developed world. I feel your critics do not credit you with the complexity of your thinking and feel much that is now labelled as 'Leach style' would appall you. You criticised much 'traditional' pottery in Japan as debased and recognised that the educated contemporary potter has to accept the position of artist. What then does this imply? If art is to have vitality, it must address the imperatives of the time in which it is made. This may oblige us to resift the spoil heaps of history, for what may have significance for one generation may not be the same for another. You are one of few great thinkers on ceramics who has committed thoughts to words. We miss out if we cannot get beyond your particular ideology, a product of its time.

We might benefit from thinking about what tradition could mean and how history might propel us into our future or trap us as slaves.

Best wishes
Sebastian Blackie

Banner, spring festival, Tokoname

To: Bernard Leach <bleach@ceramicheaven.com>
From: Sebastian Blackie <black@restlessearth.co.uk>

Subject: *Free, Forty, Five, Sex and Seven*

Dear Mr Leach

Attitudes in Japan to sex, gender and nudity I found difficult to understand. I saw no public displays of physical affection and no public display of nudity. No naked bodies in newspapers or magazines. No pornographic magazines, endemic in Europe, except for the sex 'manga' (cartoon drawings) which are read openly and portray extraordinary violence. Interestingly, the manga drawings exclude the genitals (although there are strange picture bubbles, which suggest what's going on without being explicit) whereas the historical 'erotic' prints are the opposite; concentrating on the genitals, sometimes, with the rest of the body fully clothed.

A woman who owned a clearly exclusive gallery in Nara came to the Cherry Blossom Viewing Party. She hung around on the periphery uninvited by Koie to join; to the incredulity of a Spaniard who kept jumping up to give her food and drink. He said, 'in Spain the woman is the prima donna'. In Mashiko, the wife of the generous young couple who put us up for the night retired to leave the men to drink. In a karaoke bar in

Cherry blossom viewing party, Kamiyahagi

Kamiyahagi one guy (the only woman present was the owner) kept comparing his virility with the bamboo shoot – strange as we were eating sliced bamboo shoot at the time.

I noticed in Japan pots are sold in sets of five. Is this to do with the asymmetrical aesthetic associated with the Orient or a reflection of a society, which does not operate as we do in terms of couples?

Sarah and I visited an exhibition in the UK of the Japanese photographer Araki. Most of the gallery was given over to a mass of small, sexually explicit, black and white prints, but at the entrance there were five huge, colour prints of flowers. In our culture we tend to forget that flowers are sex organs.

Traditional Japanese art is rich in subtle visual, sexual metaphor as well as highly-explicit images. One Shinto shrine has a huge phallus carved from a tree trunk. It is interesting that this would be unthinkable in a Christian church yet we happily accept the image of a man being tortured on a cross. On my second day in Japan I saw a Gothic-style church in Toyota; Shimada (Koie's assistant) said it was a 'love temple', meaning a brothel. At the spring festival in Tokoname I saw a banner with a swastika on it – Shimada said it was the sign for a temple. How misguided one can be when trying to make sense of another culture.

Koie gave me a birthday party in the last exhausting week of my visit. A soba noodle party (nothing sober about it). About 40 people came. As the chief guest I was honoured to be first in the open-air hot tub followed by about seven drunken, naked, singing men and one lone, American woman. You wrote that as a young man in Japan you fled when you discovered that you were to share a bath with a group of young women. Both cultures seem to have changed since then.

During my 40 days in Japan I think I survived by not trying to understand the culture, I became child-like, and paradoxically found a freedom to question my own culture.

Best wishes
Sebastian Blackie

To: Bernard Leach <bleach@ceramicheaven.com>
From: Sebastian Blackie <black@restlessearth.co.uk>

Subject: *No Ware*

Dear Mr Leach

I remember that your first introduction to ceramics was attending a raku party in Tokyo. I have read that before raku was given its title it was known as 'Now Ware'. This implies cutting-edge as well as spontaneously reflecting the moment, which is appropriate for such an immediate firing technique. Raku in 16th century Japan was made as an expression of nothingness, an idea that still seems extraordinarily contemporary. You have written that you feel the most beautiful pots come from a tradition of non-egotistical makers – unknown craftsmen. But what is the contemporary maker to do? Once we have eaten from the tree of knowledge we have to keep eating; replacing naivety with a philosophy. So much contemporary work seems to fall between the two.

Work from the past often has an authority and distinctiveness that seems to come from being of its time and place. Pots made from local materials meeting a local need – forms reflective of local customs and foods. The tea cup and the tea bowl reveal two very different cultures that go far beyond the objects themselves. Today, in our vagabond society, we are obliged to be consciously knowing because we are offered so many different opportunities. What we make, how we make it, with what, and where – all these things have to be thought about. The fact that we are working in such a permanent medium is in itself an issue. This choice gives us no choice but to think. To fire at all is problematic, but to fire with kilns made of paper (as I do) is a decision we need to consider.

In the past we have had an 'age of reason'. I believe we have entered the 'age of identity'. Who we are is no longer a given. We are surrounded, on the one hand, by the dangers of over-identification with groups that threaten the whole, and on the other by rootlessness, which inhibits our ability to grow.

When I was in Japan, I was deeply attracted to their approach to ceramics but it seemed pointless to me for an Occidental to make Oriental-style tea bowls. Paradoxically, I think I learnt little about the Japanese but a great deal about myself. At Koie's I chose not to use any of the wonderful glazes in the studio but signed the work using toothpaste I had brought from home; in the heat of the kiln it melted to form a glaze – East meets West!

I often find it difficult to describe to others what I make but I think now I will call it 'no ware'. It is a sort of rhyming slang for work that is 'knowing', self-aware and work that does not belong to one place, or 'nowhere'. It also makes reference to the paradoxical concept of nothingness. In many ways I think these issues of identity are the subject of my work which inform how it is made as much as what it is.

Best wishes
Sebastian Blackie

'Occidental' tea bowl. PHOTO BY SALLY EDWARDS

To: Bernard Leach <bleach@ceramicheaven.com>
From: Sebastian Blackie <black@restlessearth.co.uk>

Subject: *Making Sense*

Dear Mr Leach

I think I got some sense of the crafts from quite an early age. Perhaps I was about ten years old when my father showed me a book called *The English Country Craftsman* by Thomas Hennell. It contained meticulous, descriptive drawings. I remember the cooper, the blacksmith, the rope-maker and basket maker. I later on realised that the potter was Michael Cardew at Winchcombe; how many of the other craftsmen had a classics degree from Oxford? Hennell had been a school friend of my father and had cycled around England in the 1920s recording working craftsmen with pen and pencil. He was lost, missing in action, while fighting the Japanese in Malaya. I looked for the book when we cleared our family home but, like its author, there was no trace.

In the 1920s I imagine there would have been a sense that although under threat, the traditional crafts could be saved and that after the industrial killing of the Great War they should be saved. That the rural crafts were an expression of wholesomeness and Englishness. I remember we had a wooden bowl my father said he had bought from two 'bodgers'* working on a pole lathe in the beech woods of Berkshire. I have a hand-beaten copper tray he also acquired at this period, although I do not know its provenance. My father innocently revealed his relationship with these artefacts when he crudely punched a hole in the tray in order to hang it on the wall.

For my father they were props or symbols. A representation of a romantic obsession with the English countryside.

Thinking back, my involvement with clay was also visceral but more physical and particular. When the wind was in a northeasterly direction we could smell the London Brick Company's kilns 20 miles away near Peterborough; a strange, slightly sweet smell, a kind of earthy flatulence. Our home was 400

Yew forest, Sussex

years old and had previously been a pub. The garden was full of broken pottery: blue and white transfers on white china, polished brown salt glaze beer bottles, lead glazed and naked earthenware and hundreds of clay pipes like bleached bones from a long dead bird. We occasionally found matching pieces and tried to imagine the original whole, from the partially reconstructed. It was perhaps my first experience of the eloquence of absence and the power of suggestion. I am able to recall the taste of dry earth as I grasped the bowl of the pipe and sucked on the short fragmented stem.

I had taken my first breath of clay!

Best wishes
Sebastian Blackie

* Bodgers are men who work in the forest turning wood to make rough furniture. 'Roughly worked' has become to be known as 'badly worked' as in a 'bodged' or 'botched' job. The word derives from badger. Like the badger, the bodger goes into the wood by day and comes out of the wood at night. I am sure you agree, Mr Leach, that the Japanese have not lost an appreciation of the bodged aesthetic.

To: Bernard Leach <bleach@ceramicheaven.com>
From: Sebastian Blackie <black@restlessearth.co.uk>

Subject: *Basket Case*

Dear Mr Leach

There is a theory that pottery was first discovered by the accidental burning of a clay-lined basket when man began to settle and work the earth in Neolithic times. Perhaps the spirit of this first pot, once broken, was passed into subsequent pots by adding its crushed remains to the clay. This filler, or 'grog', would have made the new pots better able to withstand thermal shock; a ritual with a practical outcome.

Gaston Bachelard in *The Psychoanalysis of Fire,* points out that it is unlikely fire was discovered as a result of analytical thought. He proposes that a stick, rubbed in the grove of another, producing smouldering heat and eventually spurting fire, was the result of a sexual reverie. He offers numerous texts, which demonstrate a subconscious association between fire and sex, and in so doing suggests that our myths and legends provide evidence of actual events.

For example, the story of Cain and Abel is, in the view of Bruce Chatwin, a struggle for land usage between the nomad and the agriculturist at the beginning of the Neolithic period. At that time the vessel of the nomad, the lightweight gathering basket, is sacrificed to make the vessel of the settler, the heavy clay pot in which grain may be stored or cooked. If we continue to interpret the Biblical story through Chatwin's eyes, we see Cain's relationship to the land changes. His punishment for fratricide is to wander the

Mould, paper and copper wire

earth in his brother's footsteps. When we walk in the footsteps of others we must adopt their stride. We then begin to feel what they felt. But Cain was a vagabond, i.e. his relationship with the land was opportunistic and exploiting. He eventually established the first city, a man-made world, thereby effectively severing all ties to the earth (or at least creating that illusion).

The environment of the contemporary ceramic artist is psychologically, and often actually, the city. We work with materials, processed and packaged by the supplier, that have any emotional relationship with the landscape removed. But perhaps, at least in the developed world, it is the possibility of re-establishing a relationship with the earth and her natural forces that is now the ceramic imperative.

The convoluted process of weaving and then destroying paper moulds, beautiful in themselves, to make clay vessels, is about the journey not the destination. Taking a short cut is to cheat oneself out of an experience. The significance, if there is one, is in the act of making. The clay becomes an imprint of something else, a shadow, an absence, a kind of memory. It records the ritual that gave it birth and it is seriously absurd.

I have been weaving vessels with rolls of newspaper then lining them with clay which is then fired. It is a form of madness.

Best wishes
Sebastian Blackie

Earthenware pot formed in paper mould by the author

Subject: *Relative Values*

Dear Mr Leach

I recently went to my aunt's funeral, the last of my parents' generation. It was a meeting of relatives, perhaps for the last time, who will each take away some portion of my aunt's possessions. It felt strange to feel ties to these people when our lives seem so different. I told one that I had heard air traffic control (the computer) was down, he thought I was talking about the stock market!

Ceramics is rich with paradox – fragile, yet able to survive thousands of years. We know that the act of making it permanent is contributing to the planet's destruction. It has been produced in vast abundance yet its tactile intimacy can link us to an individual from a distant culture. For so many makers there is a spiritual dimension to their work yet what could be more material than clay?

I remember attending Michael Cardew's funeral. He was buried in the clay. It rained hard that day; he was a real 'mud and water man'. Soon after, we cremated my father. The rituals of death are very close to the rituals of potting. In Christian/Judaic culture attitudes to ceramics are mixed. Adam was modelled from the mixing of the earth's dust with God's spit (a wonderful metaphor for semen) yet Judas' blood money was used to buy the potters field to bury the dead. I have often wondered whether the different status of ceramics between Japan and here is due to our different religious traditions, which we inherit whether we wish to or not. The Shinto deity is in things: rocks, trees, water; ours is invisible, pure, non-material. Traditionally in the Western end of Eurasia we ascribe value to materials such as glass and gold, which express something of this material-less-ness. The translucency and whiteness of porcelain also expresses a feeling of 'not of this earth'. The crafts of Japan seem like a prayer in material form.

After my divorce, deeply in debt, I considered selling my Hans Coper pot, knowing I could never replace it. I took it to London to be valued. Afterwards, drained by the auction houses' rapacious interest, I went to the British Museum in search of solace. In the Egyptian gallery I was drawn to a stone tablet. Commissioned 'for eternity' in Mephosis by King Shibaka, it was carved, in stunningly precise hieroglyphics, to record the origins of the universe. The text was worn away in the centre and superimposed with a rough spoke-like structure made by crudely chipping at the basalt. The museum label said 'subsequently used for grinding corn'. My need for material and, what Primo Levi calls spiritual food, was answered. I felt simultaneously free from the need to sell and the fear of loss by selling. I still have the pot, now financially worthless as my second wife accidentally smashed it. In fact, it cost money to repair.

When I got home from the funeral Anita Besson phoned to say that Koie had offered to pay if I needed an operation on my back.

Best wishes
Sebastian Blackie

Scarecrows, Suffolk, UK

To: Bernard Leach <bleach@ceramicheaven.com>
From: Sebastian Blackie <black@restlessearth.co.uk>

Subject: *Boredom*

Dear Mr Leach

I grew up in monochrome 1950s Britain when children permanently wore wellingtons or sandals. Our parents had won the war and we had inherited the sunny uplands they had fought for. By day we children also owned the deserted army camp on the edge of our village with its rank, urine stench and condom-strewn air raid shelters; we had a playground we would never surrender. We swooped and banked, arms akimbo, spitting bullets from the back of our throats. We were the few.

We made things: dens, dens on the ground, in trees and attics, or excavated, Colditz-like, under our neighbour's house. I made a helicopter, the rotorblades were floorboards 'removed' from the corner of my bedroom and crudely nailed to my father's lawn mower. Later, in my teens, I turned the same lawnmower into a potter's wheel. It was a bad case of re-inventing the wheel.

We had our own language. We greeted each other with a prehensile 'woo-up' to swap comics with gripping yarns. We made reference to things we had no conception of 'Who do you think you are? Picasso?'. We believed that a '42-er' was a conker that had genuinely survived as many fights or (more interestingly) had acquired its score by accumulating the status of others it had beaten. A mindset which may have informed the approach to sexual relations in the decade to follow.

Shack, Rottnest Island

Barn and cornfield

My parents owned a Dormobile – a deeply compromised vehicle with the appearance of a Vietnamese pot-bellied pig. Each summer from the mid-1950s onward we invaded Europe in the Dormobile to be broiled and deafened hour after sleepless hour as we trundled across the hot, flat landscape of northern France.We were imprisoned in this uninsulated tin box until lunchtime when my father would park in the corner of some foreign field. We would stagger out like Alec Guinness in *The Bridge over the River Kwai* to eat bread made of crust and warm air, with cheese that had suspiciously changed its shape since purchase only hours before. Sometimes we would stop at amazing places: castles and cathedrals, the grotto at Lourdes and the prehistoric paintings in the cave at Lascaux. I realise now that the hours in the hellhole of the Dormobile were as important to the development of my imagination as the places we visited. The discomfort of the prison-like Dormobile provided a fertile ground in which ideas sown during the brief experience of freedom could flourish.

As an adult I find my better ideas often emerge during the tedium of travel as if born of boredom.

Best wishes
Sebastian Blackie

To: Bernard Leach <bleach@ceramicheaven.com>

From: Sebastian Blackie <black@restlessearth.co.uk>

Subject: *Gifts*

Dear Mr Leach

An analyst friend told me of a client whose recurrent nightmare of a bird defecating on her head as she sang suggested to the analyst that the singer should give up her career as a talented performer. He resisted this, as it seemed wrong for her not to use her gift. Eventually the woman took his advice and became content.

There is something disturbing about unused gifts and something unresolved about unwanted gifts.

When a gift is truly given its ownership is unconditional. The singer's voice is her own without obligation to use it to give pleasure to others. Presents, however, are often not gifts but tokens of a desire to receive. They create obligation; they demand a response. It seems to me that they are often coded

The Pinnacles,
Western Australia

The Pinnacles, Western Australia

requests, often indecipherable to the recipient. With such light straws we break each others backs.

We are surrounded by gifts. Some we are ready to accept, others we choose to ignore or fail to recognise. The Neolithic farmer received the gift of fired clay as pottery because this form added value to his life. The same fired clay beneath the hunter's fire may have been used as pigment. What is good for the farmer would be a burden to the hunter. The indigenous Australians used a limited range of tools. It seems to me to be a sign of high intelligence not only to uniquely invent/recognise something as aerodynamically sophisticated as the boomerang but also to only acquire what you need. It is painful to see a drunken Aborigine squatting among the glinting towers of Perth on the shore of Western Australia's vast, flat expanse.

When writing a practical book it seems important not to demand that the knowledge you are giving is used in the same way as you use it. As they say in New Zealand, '*Ka mate koe i te kai hikareti*' (your smoking can harm others). I find it exciting that toothpaste will make glaze. You, Mr Leach, may not.

Best wishes
Sebastian Blackie

Glinting towers, Melbourne

To: Bernard Leach <bleach@ceramicheaven.com>
From: Sebastian Blackie <black@restlessearth.co.uk>

Subject: *Hard Ground*

Dear Mr Leach

I was given a hard time in Denmark when I read out my message 'Gifts'. It was felt I reinforced the stereotypical white branding of Aboriginal people as alcoholics – not only do we steal their land but go on to appropriate their identity. It is uncomfortable to be told such things and tempting to either reject the criticism or find some other way to evade it. I am aware that I tread difficult ground when exploring the representation of experiences which are not directly my own, yet feel it would be a form of betrayal to have avoided the territory.

It happened this summer doing a residency at Denmark's Museum of International Ceramic Art, which culminated in a seminar on the subjects of architecture and sculpture. Several artists from around the world had been invited to make a work for the park in which the centre is located. My piece was about 'home', or rather the loss of home as a psychological space. Home is our primary experience of architecture, and as such, a space deeply charged with poetic meaning. The piece is called 'Wall'.

I used cardboard wine boxes as moulds to produce a series of blocks from local brick clay. They have a strong ceramic quality but also show the corrugations from the card, speaking of both the discarded and the permanent. The choice of cardboard imagery links to its use, in cities, by homeless people to make temporary shelter. The blocks were fired *in situ* with cardboard kilns after which they were destined for burial; a ritualised returning of the earth to itself to became an ambiguous foundation both literally and metaphorically. I arranged the blocks in the two most basic building forms – rectangle and circle. I was reminded of the circular Iron Age houses I visited in Cornwall and the wonderful sense of security I felt inside the reconstructed house with its stone walls and thatched roof. But the idea for laying out the work in a circle came from the site. When I was looking for a location I found some grass of a different tone in circular patterns; they seemed quite mysterious, almost magical, until one day of summer rain. I then discovered they were made by fungi.

The work is not site-specific but tries to be site-sensitive, developing in quite an unexpected way. On the edge of the park is a social housing estate for immigrants, refugees and ethnic Danes, once Vikings who maybe lost a focus on who to fight. It looks like a place of black eyes. By UK standards it is good, well maintained with plenty of space and equipment for children to play, but you cannot lose the smell of the ghetto so easily. I felt we invaded their space – good intentions but born of poverty.

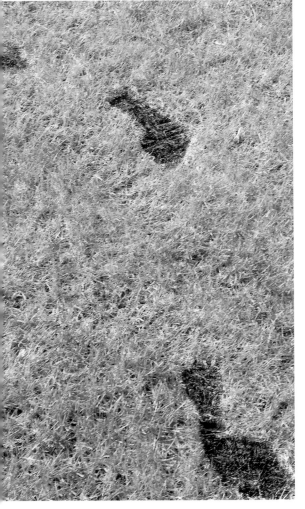

My response was to make a set of naked clay feet with which, Raku-like, I planned to brand the grass, making a trail that ran from the housing past the art to the town. I hoped it would work as an invitation to take ownership. Something that could be taken quite lightly which in time will fade.

But the feet cracked after a few steps and the blocks could not be interred as planned. The feet had been over fired and the drought had made the ground impenetrable.

Best wishes
Sebastian Blackie

P.S. Nicole e-mailed today to say that two of the other artists' work had been vandalised, blown up with powerful fireworks. It must be horrid to have your work treated in this way, but, at the risk of sounding a smart ass, it does draw attention to the responsibility to represent a community to itself; which is a major function of public art.

Branded footprints, Guldagergaard, Denmark

41

To: Bernard Leach <bleach@ceramicheaven.com>
From: Sebastian Blackie <black@restlessearth.co.uk>

Subject: *Learner*

Dear Mr Leach

There are several sources from which the idea for newspaper kilns began. Of particular importance, however, was seeing a Nigerian bush firing. Two potters who had never previously left their village were flown, together with their materials, to the UK to demonstrate. They had extraordinary composure in what must have been an utterly alien environment. They took great care to preheat their pots on the ground on which the kiln was built. Smouldering guinea corn husks (similar looking to sweet corn husks) were placed inside the pots, which quickly became too hot to handle. In due course the pots were removed and replaced with a thin layer of wood. It seems the potters were warming/drying the ground as well as their work. The pots were then stacked, rim down, on the wood, a few sticks were added and then covered first with a layer of guinea husks and finally with a layer of hay. The kiln was lit in several places igniting the hay, which quickly formed a fine, dense ash that seemed to contain the heat, generated by the slower burning corn husks and wood. The potters took great care to maintain this layer of ash throughout the firing, patching any holes with straw whose more open structure quickly burnt and was assimilated by the hay ash. The potters normally fire at dusk when the wind drops, the firing taking about two hours in total.

Do you think it is right to assume that this kind of firing was refined long ago and has remained essentially unchanged for centuries? If so, it seems likely in a poor society that anything extraneous would have been removed and that every element of the firing contributes to its success. For example, the use of four different fuels which, it seems to me, generate and contain the heat as well as regulate the air.

The bush kiln makes me think that, in many cases, the simpler the technology the greater is the skill required which in turn develops observation and a deep understanding of materials. Hunting with a bow and arrow not only requires more skill to be accurate than a telescopic rifle, but also must be done at much closer range requiring a deeper understanding of the prey. I believe one firing with a paper kiln will teach more than 100 firings in an electric kiln.

Best wishes
Sebastian Blackie

Bonfire firing by Nigerian bush potters, Aberystwyth, Wales, UK

Subject: *Fact and Fiction*

Dear Mr Leach

You asked me to explain how paper kilns are made. They are made by rolling sheets of newspaper into long, slightly conical, straws that are then woven to form a hollow basket in which pottery can be fired. When lit, the paper initially carbonises due to the compactness of the material. As the kiln burns the heat creates a draft of air causing the carbonised paper to glow with an intense, short flame in a similar way to blowing on a barbecue. Some of this heat is trapped inside the hollow structure and accumulates to provide sufficient temperatures to convert clay into ceramic or to melt materials such as glass, aluminium and copper.

The straws are made by laying flat three pages of a broadsheet newspaper slightly off-set. The paper is then rolled from one of the corners, initially between finger and thumb, then with the flat of the right hand using the left to prevent the straw from unravelling. Once a straw has been established it naturally forms a conical structure, which can be secured with a small piece of masking tape. Starting the roll can be difficult. Dampening the fingers on a wet sponge or using a short length of dry spaghetti will help. Once a number of straws have been made it is possible to form a continuous length of rolled paper by inserting the narrow end into the open end of each straw.

There are a large number of weaving techniques that can be used to make paper kilns. One of the simplest is to make a series of rings, of varying diameter, which stack on top of each other to form a beehive-like structure. These rings are made by initially joining three or four straws as described above and bending them to form a ring so that one end remains free producing a shape like a number '9'. Bending the straws locks them together. The tail of the 9 is then twisted round the ring with new straws progressively being added to the tail to allow the twisting process to continue until the ring

Rolling paper

Weaving a kiln

ABOVE AND BELOW, RIGHT:

*Different stages of
the paper kiln firing*

has become about as thick as an adult's wrist. The loose tail is then pushed through the matrix of twisted straws and pulled tight to prevent it unravelling.

The rings may be loosely stacked on top of each other but greater stability in the firing is obtained if the rings are 'sewn' together using paper straws rolled from single sheets of newspaper. Galvanised or copper wire can also be used but will not, of course, contribute heat to the firing. Once made, the kiln is packed and lit from the top. Initially long flames are produced which may crack the work unless it is preheated and an appropriate body has been used. The flames shorten as the paper is carbonised; this is when the significant heat is generated which accumulates inside the kiln firing the work. The whole process takes about 60 minutes. Several factors influence the final temperature: evenness of construction, weather conditions etc. but the total weight of fuel is very significant. To achieve 1000°C (1832°F) I find I need about 8kg (18lb) which is approximately 200 newspaper sheets of 60cm x 40cm (24in. x 16in.) size. I will e-mail you again, as there is much more to say.

My dictionary describes 'fiction' as something invented or imagined. The paper kilns are both imagined and invented.

Best wishes
Sebastian Blackie

To: Bernard Leach <bleach@ceramicheaven.com>
From: Sebastian Blackie <black@restlessearth.co.uk>

Subject: *Weaving Facts*

▶ Attachment: **Newspaper Kilns**

Dear Mr Leach

Further to my 'Fact and fiction' message, I have found that the newspaper kilns work most effectively if they are woven as evenly as possible, i.e. that the gaps between the paper straws are small and of similar size. A large gap in the lower half of the kiln will draw most of the air to it leaving other areas with poor combustion. A gap in the upper half will allow heat to escape too quickly. There are a number of basket weaving techniques I have used to produce an even structure:

Coiling

Coiling requires two long lengths of paper 'rope', one thick and the other thin. Loop the thick 'rope' to make a circle the diameter you want the base of your kiln to be. Secure this with the end of the thin rope and continue by adding a second loop of thick rope on top of the first while binding the two together with the thin rope. This spiral grows to form a cylinder, which should gently taper-in until the volume has been finally closed up producing a shape rather like a stubby bullet. To pack the kiln, either place the work in a cardboard tube with holes cut out and place your kiln over this, or make your kiln in two sections securing the top half once the work has been placed in the bottom half.

To make the thick rope, use paper straws as described in my previous e-mail 'Fact and fiction'. Secure three together with tape and plate adding more straws as you go. A rope of 24m (79ft) will make a kiln 65cm (26in.) high with a 45cm (18in.) diameter at the base. The thin rope uses straws made from single sheets of newspaper and is best constructed as building progresses. The coiling method is particularly useful where one has difficulty making tightly rolled straws as the plaiting and subsequent binding of the rope will compact the paper so necessary for carbonisation.

Warp and weft

This method also uses paper straws. First mark out the circumference of your kiln on a soft surface such as a lawn (a bag of soft clay will do). Then plant your straws about 80mm (3in.) apart, about three to each hole, so that they are held firm. These are the warp or stakes. The kiln is then constructed by weaving single straws between them, adding in extra straws as you go. These are known as the weft or weavers. The stakes need to be considerably more robust than the weavers. This can be achieved by using glossy magazine paper, which will also burn more slowly than newspaper, helping to maintain the integrity of the structure during firing. It is a beautiful way to make a kiln and produces a very even matrix but the wall of the kiln is quite thin, generating limited heat.

I am sure there must be other weaving techniques one could use and other ways to prepare the paper which is less time consuming. I will do some experiments.

There is more to tell you about newspaper kilns, which I will send as an attachment.

Best wishes
Sebastian Blackie

Weaving kilns, Hove Museum, UK

▼ *Newspaper Kilns*

My self-imposed brief with paper kilns is to make them work without resorting to conventional ceramic equipment. I have therefore always fired the work raw.

The biggest problem has been to start the firing sufficiently slowly not to blow up the work but then in the latter stages have enough draft to burn the carbon well to gain temperature. A suitable clay and the use of preheating described in my e-mail on p.82 'Yalc' (clay spelt backwards if you hadn't realised) are ways to deal with the problems associated with the start of the firing. The cardboard/slip/paper skin described in 'Pen to Paper' (on p.56) is a way to increase draft. I think, however, it may be useful to describe some of the other ideas I have used.

Paper kilns are substantially lighter than conventional kilns. As a result, it is possible to suspend the kiln and preheat the work over a fire. To do this I have used a paper chain, made in the same way as the kiln, which is so strong it will bear my weight (convict potters take note). I have had some success with this, but it does mean that the kiln lights first at the bottom if lowered onto the fire. The flames then pass into the pack much sooner than when the kiln is lit from the top – somewhat defeating the object. I must try some more experiments.

To preheat the work I have pre-packed it in a pierced, cylindrical drum made of card which is warmed in a conventional kitchen oven (this needs careful monitoring to avoid a house fire). Alternatively, a small chamber made from chicken wire covered with wet paper and heated with a gas poker can be used. The work can then be quickly brought to the kiln and the firing started before there is a chance for it to cool and reabsorb moisture.

The use of different papers can be significant. Shiny magazine papers burn much more slowly producing better heat work i.e. time for the heat to actually penetrate and fire the body of clay. Just as with cooking food, long periods at low temperatures may be much more thorough than brief, high

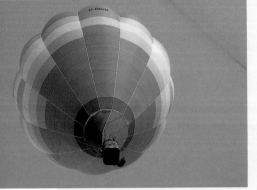

temperatures. Magazines are much cleaner to roll but their smaller format means that it takes longer to produce enough to build a kiln. A combination of news and magazine paper is a good compromise.

I hope one day to make a flying kiln using the waste heat to power a hot air balloon and exploit the kiln's lightness and disposability. Hopefully, as it rises it will meet greater wind speeds, which should increase the rate of burning which will then subside for the cooling as the balloon begins to meet wind velocity. By calculating the distance the kiln will travel and the wind direction it might be possible to deliver the work direct to the gallery!

Firing, Anseong Ceramic Festival, Korea

To: Bernard Leach <bleach@ceramicheaven.com>

From: Sebastian Blackie <black@restlessearth.co.uk>

Subject: *Earth, Air, Fire and Water*

Dear Mr Leach

Many years ago I built a kiln with flying buttresses. As a child I learnt best by making: a secret tunnel under our neighbour's house, a fish trap using the garden fence, a helicopter from a lawnmower and some floor boards. In some desperation my father subscribed, on my behalf, to magazine called *Knowledge*. In *Knowledge* I discovered what I now know is an example of symbiosis. I read it is possible to boil water in a paper vessel over a candle. I intend to use this principle to make a floating kiln at the Appledore festival.

I plan to make the 'boat' from cardboard covered with paper and slip and to attach fins, which will cause the boat to spin with the wind. This should mean that the paper kiln will burn much more evenly. Wind produces a hotter firing but it makes the kiln unstable due to one-sided burning.

So often knowledge inhibits play instead of informing it. I used to fire in conventional saggars; heavy, slow and expensive to fire. I now make saggars with paper and slip (an idea that came from Aline Favre's paper/wood kiln). These can be fired up to 10 times at 1300°C (2372°F). They are quick to make, can be used immediately without drying or firing and they have almost no thermal mass which means they can be fired very fast.

I use a cylinder of cardboard as the former which means I can tailor-make the saggar to fit each pot, this is then coated with about 15 layers of newspaper and slip. The saggar is then placed on a kiln shelf and packed with pots and sawdust.

I usually soak the kiln at about 500°C (932°F) until the sawdust has fully carbonised and to allow the heat to penetrate the pack. At 1300°C (2372°F) I soak anything between 30 minutes and three hours then crash cool to 800°C (1472°F) by opening the door.

This kind of firing leaves a distinctive whitish line across the work. Above the line the variation of colour results from different degrees of reduction and re-oxidisation, fly-ash glazing etc. Below the line the colour is the soft, sometimes lustrous, blue-black of impregnated carbon. The line, I believe, is the result of sawdust continuing to burn as the kiln cools, exposing the impregnated carbon to air.

I am taking a big risk at Appledore by doing something untried; but isn't it more fun to be part of an experiment than be demonstrated to?

Best wishes
Sebastian Blackie

ABOVE: *Making paper saggar*
RIGHT: *Paper saggars cooling in the kiln*

Paper saggars ready for unpacking

Saggar-fired pot by the author

To: Bernard Leach <bleach@ceramicheaven.com>
From: Sebastian Blackie <black@restlessearth.co.uk>

Subject: *Good Deal*

Dear Mr Leach

I am sorry I have not yet explained to you how cardboard kilns work. I agree it sounds a bit implausible, but through history potters have used almost anything that will burn as fuel – from animal dung to car tyres.

The principles of cardboard kilns are much the same as newspaper kilns. When lit, the cardboard, compacted under its own weight, will initially carbonise. Once this charring phase is complete, drawing air through this mass of glowing carbon generates the heat. Some of the heat accumulates in the chamber and is insulated by the layer of ash, which forms on the outer wall of the kiln.

Depriving the fuel of sufficient air to burn efficiently at the start of the firing is crucial to both newspaper and cardboard kilns. With paper kilns this is achieved by rolling and weaving. Cardboard is more resistant to bending than newspaper and requires a different design approach.

Most of the cardboard kilns I have built have used packaging material from shops, the majority being boxes. Supermarkets generate bales of the stuff daily. To prepare the fuel for building it is necessary to cut the cardboard so as to have a large quantity

Building a cardboard kiln, National College of Art and Design, Dublin, Ireland

Waste cardboard

of rectangular sheets of roughly similar dimension. The source of cardboard will determine the size but you should try to build a kiln with a wall no less than 150mm (6in.) and perhaps no more than 300mm (12in.) thick.

A simple design for cardboard kilns is to construct a form like a log cabin. Strips of cardboard, approximately 200mm (8in.) wide, are laid flat on the ground to form (in plan) a frame making a square void approximately 450mm (18in.) across. As successive layers are added a central chamber is formed. When the walls of the kiln have been built up to a height of about 600mm (24in.) the chamber is packed with work and roofed over with larger sheets of cardboard. More cardboard should be added to the roof until it is as least as thick as the walls.

When using the 'log cabin' design it is important to ensure the walls and roof are compact and consistent so that burning is fairly slow and even. Overlapping the sheets of card, in the same way builders stagger bricks when building a wall, is important to avoid vertical seams developing which will reduce the kiln's stability when firing. If the cardboard is overlapped at the corners an additional sheet per course will need to be placed in the wall between corners to maintain consistent density.

Larger kilns can be built than the one I have described but the ratio of wall thickness to chamber and the ratio of chamber width to height should be maintained. In this design the weight of the material provides the right conditions to carbonise the card, however, the taller the kiln the greater is the weight on the bottom layers. If the carbonised cardboard becomes over-compressed, air will not be drawn through the glowing wall resulting in an excessively slow firing with insufficient heat being generated.

When the kiln is built I light it at several points. This can be quite difficult but much helped if a blowlamp is used. The kiln is then left to its own devices, taking up to eight hours to fire.

It is not difficult to get ideas for other designs if you keep your eyes open. One design is based on Celtic roundhouses, which use a corbel arch. Another I call the 'bookshelf kiln' because the card is stacked vertically which should allow larger kilns to be made without the problem of compacting the card. The major advantage of cardboard kilns over newspaper kilns is that they are much quicker to build and require less skill to make. These characteristics make it relatively easy to build large kilns with a substantial volume of fuel and therefore, potentially, higher temperatures. Their major disadvantage is that they generally need more air movement to gain temperature, and during the firing can release in the wind large flakes of glowing ash which might be a fire hazard. However, this can be reduced if the kiln is covered with a cage of chicken wire.

In my experience, a process of observation and review refines this kind of simple technology. For example, I realised that large 'log cabin' kilns may be improved by stacking the lower layers of card more loosely than those near the top to counter the compression at the base from the weight of card above. Attempts to solve one problem, perhaps unsuccessfully, may open up a whole new design strategy. An example of this is making an outer cardboard skin to contain the loose card fuel. The consequence was that I gained real control of airflow. This means I can start the firing slowly, with much less risk to the work, but increase the rate of burning towards the end, which results in much higher temperatures. I will tell you more about this in my next message, 'Pen to Paper'.

Firing with recycled materials like cardboard seems to me to be more sustainable than using fossil fuel. You have to work hard physically to make the kiln and will need a good deal of card. But the card is free, encouraging experiment. A good deal in many ways.

Best wishes
Sebastian Blackie

Cardboard kilns, Research Dept., Museum of International Ceramic Art, Denmark.
PHOTO NICOLE LISTER

To: Bernard Leach <bleach@ceramicheaven.com>

From: Sebastian Blackie <black@restlessearth.co.uk>

Subject: *Pen to Paper*

▶ Attachment: **Constructing the skin of a cardboard kiln**
(and a few other bits and pieces).

Dear Mr Leach

I feel the need to write again. The Americans, at great expense, developed a pen for use in zero gravity. When they asked the Russians how they wrote in space they said they used 'a pencil'. Both solutions represent admirable human characteristics; both are creative in very different ways. I sometimes wonder why I have developed card and paper kilns when I have a perfectly good gas kiln in my workshop.

In many ways these experimental kilns have been a challenge to my practice, causing me to question why I make, as well as what, and how. It has produced by-products such as the paper saggers described in my previous 'Earth, air, fire

Wood/paper/slip kiln being placed over embers

and water' e-mail. It has led to invitations to collaborate with others from whom I have acquired new skills such as basket weaving and tinsmith pattern-making. Perhaps most important of all it has encouraged me to question the future of ceramic practice; to lift my head from the clay and look both forward and backwards in an attempt to understand where I am going.

Much of the development has made me feel stupid rather than clever. After months of thinking up elaborate solutions to a problem I can suddenly realise that I already had the simplest of answers applied elsewhere (like the Russian pencil). An example of this is the cardboard skin referred to in my previous e-mail 'Good deal' (p.53).

Years ago the Swiss potter Aline Favre described a kiln built on an open steel base where the work is surrounded with wood logs and then covered with layers of glossy magazine paper coated with slip. The kiln is initially suspended on bricks over glowing embers, which preheats the work and roasts the logs. The bricks are then removed; the wood ignites and is converted to charcoal because the paper/slip skin limits the oxygen needed for full combustion. The temperature rise during this phase is quite slow so there is little danger of damaging the clay work. The gases given off ignite outside the kiln but once the charcoal is produced, it in turn begins to burn but with a short, hot flame inside the kiln. The charcoal burns first near the base where the air is drawn in and is replaced by the charcoal above. Airflow increases as the kiln gets hotter and because the diminishing fuel offers less resistance. This in turn assists combustion and greater heat. The volume of wood used determines the final temperature and I have reached 1300°C (2372°F) in a kiln of this design. The skin not only controls the airflow but also puffs up like pastry, providing insulation.

Applying this idea to both newspaper and cardboard kilns has reduced the loss of work at the beginning of the firing and allowed me to achieve much higher temperatures. Problems of one-sided burning and premature collapse due to wind disappear, and by adding a card/slip/paper chimney, draft can be increased.

LEFT, TOP TO BOTTOM:
Wood/paper/slip kiln – charring cycle

Wood/paper/slip kiln at top temperature

I enclose an attachment explaining how the cardboard armature for the skin is calculated. Once made it is covered with about 20 layers of newspaper painted with slip. It may be necessary to allow the layers to partially dry to prevent the card from becoming soggy, however the kiln does not need to dry out before use. Do you think this is a 'Pen or Pencil' solution?

Best wishes
Sebastian Blackie

▼ *Constructing the skin of a cardboard kiln (and a few other bits and pieces).*

Moulding three-dimensional forms from sheet material using techniques such as vacuum forming and pressing is common enough, but doing this by construction requires a practical use of mathematics, which achieved great sophistication in the hands of the 19th century tinsmith. Just as I have learnt ways of dealing with dyslexia, I have also gained some confidence by approaching mathematics through practice rather than theory.

The form I require for the body of my kiln is a pointed dome, in section a lancet arch. To make, I first decide on height and width and draw this to scale with the curving wall as an elevation. I then divide up the axis into equal sections usually every 25cm (10in.) for a 2m (78in.) high kiln. With a compass I can then measure the radius of each section which is recorded as a series of circles in plan. The plan is then divided into 12 equal segments with the help of a compass. Taking one of these, I measure the distance between the edges of the segment where each circle intersects. These measurements can then be scaled up and drawn out on a template.

The template is used to cut 12 segments of card that can be joined with parcel tape to produce the skin. I use corrugated card and alternate the template, head to tail, to ensure that the corrugation runs vertically up each segment as well as to get as many segments as possible from each sheet of card.

With the chimney I do not bother to calculate in this way and find a cylinder is easily constructed to fit.

When designing any draft kiln, it is useful to remember that air doubles its volume every 366°C (690°F). Thus, air entering the kiln through a hole, say 10 × 10cm (4 × 4in.) will need a chimney that has an area of 800cm^2 (128in.^{2}) if it is not to choke at 1000°C (1832°F) (and twice that at 1300°C/2372°F). Although the height of a chimney will increase draft this will make little difference if it is too narrow; in fact the chimney will become hotter exacerbating the problem. So far my chimneys have been slightly less than the chamber height so as not to place too much weight on the structure. A higher chimney would increase the rate of combustion (and thus potentially the temperature), which, if excessive, can always be reduced by 'bleeding' (making a small hole near the chimney's base, which dissipates the pull on the chamber).

I use two methods to introduce air for combustion, either a 20mm (8in.) hole cut into each panel about 10cm (4in.) from the base, or if conditions are suitable I bury a horizontal cardboard tube into the ground connected to the surface with short sections of the same tube which delivers the air to the core of the kiln. In the latter case, in order to light the kiln, I split the tube and lay a fuse of paraffin-soaked sawdust and crumbled firelighters before replacing the top section and burying with earth. To establish some draft I ignite crumpled newspaper in the chimney and light the sawdust. The flame is quickly drawn underground and lights the fuel. Just as water can be made to flow uphill against its natural tendency by means of a siphon, so flames can be drawn down through the sucking action of a chimney – fascinating.

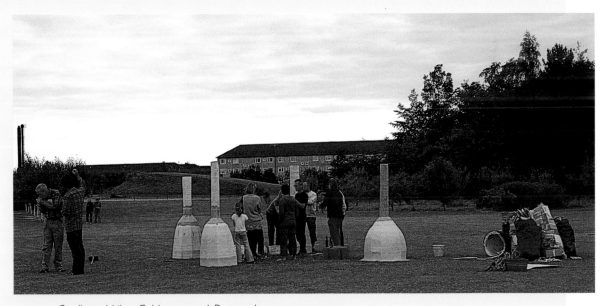

Cardboard kilns, Guldagergaard, Denmark. PHOTO NICOLE LISTER

To: Bernard Leach <bleach@ceramicheaven.com>
From: Sebastian Blackie <black@restlessearth.co.uk>

Subject: *Going Back*

Dear Mr Leach

The results of my scan came through and it seems I have a slipped disc with collateral damage. The experience of the scan was very interesting. I had to remain absolutely still for, I was told, 20 minutes, in a position I found very painful. The confined featureless space and the intrusive mechanical sound of the scanner produced a form of sensory deprivation. Although I knew it would come to an end I could not judge how long I was inside. The intensity of the pain and the passing of time existed without dimension. As I lay trapped in the tunnel of the scanner I felt as if I was going through a kind of rebirth. I struggled to be optimistic but felt intense loss for my past life.

I realise this injury will quite profoundly affect my approach to life. It requires me to reshape my self-image. Sandy Brown phoned to discuss my project at the Appledore festival. We agreed I could not make an exhibition but should try to direct the building of kilns with college students doing the physical work. This is so different to my hands-on approach. I begin to understand how I must rethink my making and teaching strategies.

In my first year of graduation I taught pottery to people who had recently gone blind. One new student convinced herself of her own uselessness because her wonky pot did not resemble a Wedgwood vase.

Firing a cardboard kiln, Appledore, Devon, UK

As we talked I discovered that she was missing her son who used to describe to her the birds feeding outside the window. When I suggested the vase might be made into a nesting box she was transformed. The criteria changed and the objective became both more realistic and closer to the reality of her emotional state. She could make something that added value to her new life. Looking back 30 years I question my advice.

The desire to remove pain is very tempting.

How can you make whole work unless you use the whole self?

Best wishes
Sebastian Blackie

To: Bernard Leach <bleach@ceramicheaven.com>

From: Sebastian Blackie <black@restlessearth.co.uk>

Subject: **Sun and Moon**

Dear Mr Leach

Appledore was great. Beautiful, sunny weather. New friends, lively conversation and, with a lot of support, two new kilns. My bad back obliges me to accept help, resulting in greater participation and a real sense of achievement as a group. Disability is a great teacher and, I think, I have become a better teacher for being disabled (I actually feel some of your best pots were done when you became blind).

We made a newspaper kiln which we floated in a boat made from cardboard covered with a few layers of slip and paper. It worked wonderfully, firing for about 70 minutes. For safety reasons we launched it on a tidal pool that meant it did not spin for long, as planned, and therefore burnt one-sided. It was so beautiful with the fire reflected on the water surrounded by an incredulous audience. It will be even better at night. The symbiosis between fire and water worked well on the base of the boat but the sides burnt through above the water-line and will require more paper and slip next time.

The cardboard kiln collapsed prematurely, due, I think, to a combination of factors. The former became soggy from the slip-covered paper and lost its structural strength. In future it will be necessary to either allow the slip to stiffen before adding extra layers or cover the card in polythene. The moisture also caused the fuel (cut sheets of card) to settle as it burnt before the outer skin had dried sufficiently for the chimney to support its own weight. This downward pressure forced the shoulder of the kiln outwards, rupturing the wall. I believe a champagne bottle-like design should work, allowing the chimney's weight to transfer more gradually to the base.

Some moisture is good, as the work is much more likely to survive if it is heated in an atmosphere just slightly less humid than the clay body. Tim, a man I met at Appledore, told me that his factory 'dries' their tiles at 180°C (356°F) under humid conditions, followed by a very rapid firing. He also told me that paper for laser printing is coated with a coarse, siliceous, kaolin that he believes could, if fired correctly, provide a permanent residue.

It is said that there is nothing new under the sun, but new materials and technologies as well as different needs and imperatives should encourage us to reappraise what we do.

I have been invited to make a number of floating, spinning, paper kilns for the opening of the new British International Clay Centre. I plan to experiment by soaking the paper in different glaze materials to see if I can get different coloured flames. I hope we can do it at night under a full moon.

Best wishes
Sebastian Blackie

Floating paper kiln, Devon, UK

To: Bernard Leach <bleach@ceramicheaven.com>
From: Sebastian Blackie <black@restlessearth.co.uk>

Subject: *Through a Glass Darkly*

Dear Mr Leach

'You would be insane if you swam in that river', I told my bad joke as we walked to Sainte Chapelle in Paris. Sainte Chapelle is on the same island as Notre Dame, tucked behind the law courts. We enter via narrow, disorientating, spiral stairs to a breathtaking vision of coloured light. A view of heaven. Instantly the spirit soars in vaulting space and my body almost collapses under the weight of my upturned head. The chapel has the highest ratio of stained glass to supporting structure of any medieval building. This glass is not about utility; it has not been made for the body but the soul.

Glaze on medieval pots is often purely ornamental, its function to enrich. In time its ability to seal the clay surface was also used but it was not until the previously unknown world of micro-organisms that glaze became assessed in terms of health. More recently, the release of toxic elements from fired glaze such as lead and barium have impacted on the range of ceramic surfaces.

We have lost:
Crazing – that wonderful network of lines that are the beauty of age, speaking of use, of life after the fire, the settling of tensions.
Crawling – blobs of round, matt, feldspar with a sheen like congealed lard, that leave the exposed clay surface wetted like a sea-washed pebble.
Matt clay glazes – leathery and wrinkled.
Flux matts – crusty, frosty ice through which dark silent water can be dimly seen.
Low alumina glazes – running green like spring streams on which strips of smoked salmon can bask.

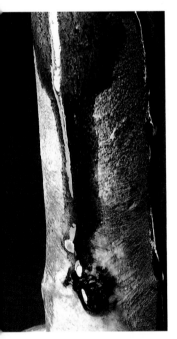

A dripping glaze (detail of author's work)

It is interesting how much a simple pot can reveal the concerns of the society that produced it. In World War II the Leach pottery made sparsely-glazed utility ware. The naked clay showed solidarity with the prevailing aesthetic of austerity but I cannot believe this small saving on wood ash contributed materially to the war effort. Today our aesthetics of use are concerned with the appearance, rather than the reality, of hygiene. That why I make glaze from toothpaste!

What evolutionary advantage has developed our ability to deny the reality we live in? In *La Grande Jatte*, Seurat applied new theories derived from optic glass, splitting white light into its component colours. People bathing in the Seine, an illusion of tranquility meticulously constructed with tiny dots. The same technology might have revealed the river teaming with bacteria. A sick joke.

Best wishes
Sebastian Blackie

Jar by Ryoji Koie

To: Bernard Leach <bleach@ceramicheaven.com>
From: Sebastian Blackie <black@restlessearth.co.uk>

Subject: *High Street Glaze*

Dear Mr Leach

You and Hamada brought back from Japan both a practical knowledge of glaze making and an appreciation of glaze quality that was quite new to the West. You have written that the two of you spent many days gathering raw materials from the Cornish countryside and testing them. Today, with the plethora of published glaze recipes and access to standardised materials, some of this pioneering spirit has gone.

Until relatively recently, potters developed glazes through empirical experiment rather than by scientific knowledge. They used locally found materials that were fired without precise temperature control using solid fuels such as wood or coal. Many cultures, such as in sub-Saharan Africa and the Americas for example, did not use glaze at all. Others, in Europe, the Middle East and the Indian subcontinent worked predominantly at low temperature using soda or lead as the flux. In China, Korea, Japan and South East Asia however, the early development of high temperature kilns enabled a much wider range of materials to melt, resulting in an extraordinary range of glazes.

Just as with cheese in France, glaze quality would have been refined from the materials available within a locality. The potters must have discovered that, for example, clay from a certain spot mixed in a certain proportion with ash from a particular plant could make a glaze without knowing what these materials contained.

We may overlook the fact that these same minerals are available in the modern urban environment but used for different purposes. The supermarket contains many products that will melt to form glaze. Toothpaste, for example, contains china clay and calcium. These products, however, are not particular to place but by brand. When fired it is obvious that not all brands are the same, but like potters in the past, toothpaste manufacturers are unwilling to share their recipes. It is clear, however, that toothpastes are high in flux producing either very runny glazes or dry crusty matts when applied thickly.

One can see that many cleaning materials probably contain salt which, when fired, produce a tell-tale halo effect. Because these products also contain other minerals, they can be significantly different from using pure salt alone. Sometimes the most unlikely products will produce interesting results. Organic materials, which may contain small quantities of glaze-making minerals should not be ignored. Some products are, in effect, already glazes or frits in an unfamiliar form. Glass fibre matting and cement for example.

Experimenting with these materials is not only a different way to explore our environment but also a creative ceramic challenge in terms of applying the material to the clay surface. What effect might shaving foam or talcum powder produce?

There is of course a risk working in this way. Common sense dictates that highly-flammable materials should not be used. Products containing toxic

A test pot with toothpaste glaze

materials will be labelled already and are wisely avoided. The most likely hazard to health is from fumes, which could be toxic, being given off during firing (as can be the case when using conventional glaze material) and care should be taken accordingly to ensure the kiln (and kiln room) is well vented. In many ways it is probably safer handling these materials than conventional ceramic materials, nevertheless it is wise to observe normal glaze room health and safety protocols. The life of electric kiln elements is shortened when organic material is burnt; however this is marginal if interspersed with 'clean' firings. Without a sound understanding of ceramic technology and knowledge of the minerals contained in the materials being used, it is unwise to use this type of glaze for utilitarian work, as soluble minerals may still be present which could leak out into food or drink.

As with all glaze experimentation, it is good practice to test small quantities first on the inside of a container to contain the melt. Kiln furniture may require additional protection with a layer of coarse sand or alumina from materials such as salt, which are highly corrosive when fired.

There are many excellent publications on glaze technology which not only explain the role of different materials but also the significance of temperature, atmosphere, firing cycles, relationship with clay body etc. This text just touches on a small aspect of glazing, more to inspire experiment than provide scholarly knowledge.

Best wishes
Sebastian Blackie

OPPOSITE: *Test piece fired to 1200°C (2192°F), using various toothpastes, plumber's paste, steel polish, brass polish, athlete's foot paste, pan cleaning powder*

To: Bernard Leach <bleach@ceramicheaven.com>
From: Sebastian Blackie <black@restlessearth.co.uk>

Subject: *Handles*

Dear Mr Leach

I have a book which was a gift to my grandmother from an unknown source in 1912. *The Woman's Book* 'contains everything a woman ought to know'. Amongst the many wifely skills it explains how to lay out a corpse. The author, however, did not appear to think that a woman ought to know about sex. The nearest reference is 'fulfilling woman's noblest mission' for which 'plenty of pure fresh air' is the highest priority.

Your publication, *The Potter's Book,* could be similarly subtitled 'contains everything a potter ought to know', although Michael Cardew would clearly not agree. Both books are practical and both assert the right way to do things; a disturbing certainty which I have difficulty identifying with. I am not suggesting we reinvent the wheel, but from time to time question what the wheel is for and whether it is taking us down an ever-deepening rut.

Take the handle. It is not just a means to lift a cup but an introduction. The handle is not confined to utility. It can play with expectation through sight and confirmation through touch. It can, for example, express ambivalence over contact with another entity.

We make handles using the method we have been taught. They look like handles and probably work as handles so we forget what they are for. Rituals can lose their meaning.

We have discarded much of the fetish behaviour described in *The Woman's Book* but we might still bring out the teapot for a guest. In the age of teabags such utensils have increasingly become tokens of value and respect. They are vessels whose prime function is to allow us to act out rituals of giving and receiving.

I have a collection of teapots. One is a small, two-cup thrown and squared piece by Randy Johnson from Minnesota. It has a snub spout and little clay strap on the lid, a finial contrasting with the generous lolling handle. The otherwise rough-cut surface is softened by a few trails of slip like a hastily decorated cake. It suggests intimacy, informality, it is charming and friendly. How different to the 18th century moulded porcelain from Newhall (see p.81). Its elongated body is further extended by a long spout at one end and stiff upright handle at the other, creating physical distance between giver and receiver. Its cool white surface is decorated with dainty flowers. It is about politeness, elegance and refinement. It has a firm grip and sense of proportion – how English!

The stifling air of social position expressed in *The Woman's Book* has gone, thank God, but the complexities of contemporary relationships are a challenge to the maker. Is it possible, I wonder, to make a feminist teapot?

Best wishes
Sebastian Blackie

Two tea bowl mug by the author

To: Bernard Leach <bleach@ceramicheaven.com>
From: Sebastian Blackie <black@restlessearth.co.uk>

Subject: *Pit*

Dear Mr Leach

We spent all afternoon in the clay pit. It felt as if the tree-lined perimeter of this man-made valley was the edge of the universe.

Clay pit, Sussex

It was one of those hot, airless summer days. It smelt of damp, warm clay mixed with the more spicy smell of crushed foliage. Bumblebees, true to their name, clumsily collected pollen from the foxgloves. Long ago the potters had found this small deposit of white clay in an area otherwise covered with iron rich earthenware; on this side a dark brick clay, across the valley to the south a plastic clay used for pot making. The former was used to build the bottle kilns that fired the pots from brown to orange, finely thrown from the latter. They decorated these with clay dug from this pit before covering with a glaze of lead and copper that fired over the white slip to a deep apple-green colour; the fruit of knowledge.

From the state of the undergrowth I would think the pit must have last been worked about 20 years before. It was difficult to tell as the potters must have left a pretty sterile environment that would have resisted the re-colonisation of plants. Recently the farmer had introduced a few Norway spruce as a crop or perhaps just in an attempt to rehabilitate this industrially created rural wilderness. They had yet to make much impact amongst the native long grasses and spindly willow herb.

During the Roman occupation of Britain, vast quantities of black fired pottery was produced in the area. The presence of several different types of clay and sand, together with the abundance of fuel from the forest, offered an ideal combination of raw materials. A navigable river that connected to the

Bottle Kilns

Thames provided a natural highway to transport heavy goods to the market of London.

When the Romans left Britain some Saxon potters reverted to the less efficient making method of coiling; something that challenges our assumption that technology progresses in a forward, linear manner. I think the most rational explanation is that throwing may just have been too productive for a post-Roman economy. That where there were no natural highways, pottery production was quickly confined to a small local market as the Roman infrastructure collapsed. Throwing arguably also represents a greater capital investment than coiling in terms of acquiring skill, equipment and time spent in refining clay to the necessary quality. I am tempted to also wonder whether a kind of nationalism was being expressed. That traditions of making might carry a cultural identity, as does song or dance. Was throwing seen as that fancy southern technique, coiling as a down-to-earth Saxon method?

There is an aspect of nationalism that is to do with feeling you belong to the earth. Perhaps it is to do with being made somewhere and dying in the same place and making your life there also.

The grass was too long for comfort and too sparse for privacy but it did not seem to matter, we existed outside normal time as we spent that hot afternoon together making love in a clay pit.

Best wishes
Sebastian Blackie

To: Bernard Leach <bleach@ceramicheaven.com>

From: Sebastian Blackie <black@restlessearth.co.uk>

Subject: *Slip of a Thing*

Dear Mr Leach

Sarah, my wife, is pregnant. It is so exciting, but when the child is 10, I, like The Beatles' song, will be 64. Since I have been writing to you I have become very conscious of my age. Some years ago I nearly died. This experience, together with the death of my parents and the birth of my other children, has profoundly affected my approach to life. A knowledge, which cannot be gained from books, that 'all things must pass'.

I grow more inclined to allow people to learn for themselves. I believe this means teaching, structure, intervention but not ownership of what is learnt which is particular to the individual. I have not been inspired to write a book before, unwilling to add to the plethora of informative literature on how to make ceramics. As a student, my tutor was one of your students, the Canadian John Reeve. He allowed me to work uninterrupted for three months then gave me a tutorial at my request in which he mostly just listened. I feel John is still teaching me. The effort of the other staff reminds me of myself washing my children's nappies – basic, necessary, and forgettable.

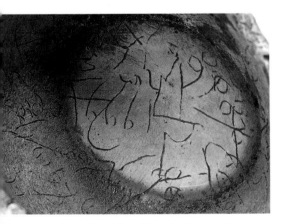

Sgraffito writing through vitreous slip

You asked me whether I use slip. There are two very different types of slip. One is the result of making, for example the water used when throwing combines with the surface of the clay in the process of formation, an embryonic fluid by which the form is delivered; surface decoration integral to the structure of making, not the subject but a means. The other is applied when the clay has partially dried. Cool liquid clay that can clothe the naked pot in its infancy. Delineating form, providing focus and contrast. It offers a visual memory in the fired work of its slippery vulnerable past. Slip is sensual and celebratory; it

Coil pot with porcelainous slip by the author

can ornament the work with pattern like a richly embroidered jacket. I am resisting writing about it. It feels too personal.

Some might find slip relevant to work fired in the card and paper kilns. Terra sigillata for example, whose colloidal particles, discovered by the ancient Greeks, responds to the variations of atmosphere natural in this type of firing. Vitreous slips containing additional flux, which are active at stoneware temperatures, may also be interesting to investigate for the same reason. With a bit of effort, information on both can be found elsewhere, but some things should not, or cannot, be passed on and are best left as private discoveries.

How often do children slip from their parent's dry, well-intentioned grip?

Best wishes
Sebastian Blackie

Tea bowl on stand; vitreous slip by the author

To: Bernard Leach <bleach@ceramicheaven.com>
From: Sebastian Blackie <black@restlessearth.co.uk>

Subject: *Tools*

Dear Mr Leach

In his novel *1984*, George Orwell points out how language conditions thought. That ideas are contingent on an appropriate vocabulary. Certainly it seems to be a common experience that we discover what we think by expressing it.

For me the process of making is like this. When I make I am exploring an idea not illustrating it. Because of this the methods, tools and clay are very important. One tool will allow me to say something that another will not.

As a student I was introduced to the potter's bow – a steel wire stretched on a frame to cut slabs. Brick makers call it a 'frog', using it to remove excess clay from a mould. I made my own bow from three lengths of wood joined with loosely fitting tongue-and-grove joints to form a shape like a squat capital 'H'. The wire is stretched between the 'legs' of the H and can be brought under tension, due to the loose joints, with a tourniquet placed on the 'arms' of the H. I found that if I used a very fine guitar string I could cut the clay with little resistance.

This tool allows me to do things with clay like no other. It can make soft clay appear hard and sharp, which, when moved, reveals the softness of the clay again, expressing its current state and anticipating its fired state. It gives a surface that looks untouched – a dramatic contrast to the surface produced by coiling or throwing. I can cut three-dimensional forms with it out of blocks of clay or make slabs with a relief pattern by moving the wire up and down as I cut. As in any ceramic forming process it works better with

Author cutting handles with a bow

some clay bodies than others. Of course, grogged clay may tear; a sticky, plastic throwing clay will tend to rejoin behind the wire cut. I use a smooth body with about 30% fine sand or grog that parts cleanly. When working this way I am particularly conscientious in preparing the clay and very aware of the alignment of the particles when I make the cut. Cracks that appear in drying or firing often originate from ignoring the microscopic structure of the clay.

I am particularly interested in making handles with this method. This signifier of holding is subverted by the untouched appearance. It looks like a handle but also it is reminiscent of the guard on a sword. It has something of the tension of shaking hands with a stranger. I make the handles by cutting a loop into a block of clay. Imagine holding a stick between your hands, arms equally extended, and then moving both hands in the same direction as if winding a crank; the stick will describe a cylinder shape. Cutting the handle is done similarly but with an elliptical motion. The excess clay is then peeled back and the handle removed and bent into shape.

This method depends on the relatively recent development of high-quality steel. Traditional techniques are incredibly useful but they are not static. Like language, we may need to add to our making vocabulary in order to communicate effectively.

Best wishes
Sebastian Blackie

P.S. A friend who played with the rock band Pink Floyd gave me a stack of guitar strings for my bow. I found out recently that the father of another friend (who works with dogs for the blind) left Pink Floyd before they were famous to get a 'proper job'. Tradition may not help us see into the future.

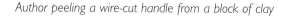

Author peeling a wire-cut handle from a block of clay

To: Bernard Leach <bleach@ceramicheaven.com>
From: Sebastian Blackie <black@restlessearth.co.uk>

Subject: *Lips*

Dear Mr Leach

As a child I was x-rayed to see whether I had swallowed a light bulb, but instead the doctor discovered a zip! Technology reveals ever more complex identities. The MRI scan of my spine required me to re-examine my self image. This new vision of internal self is a challenge to the powerful idea of vessel as metaphor for the body.

Yet the language remains. We describe the components of pots like those of ourselves – foot, belly, shoulder, neck and lip. The lip being perhaps the most potent, as it is the point of transition from outer to the interestingly unnamed, inner. In drinking vessels, the pot's lip meets our lips – the content of one vessel passes into us, another vessel. It is interesting to examine this exchange.

From the outside our lips begin with a change of skin colour. This suggests they are part of our inside. But from the inside we can feel a change in texture that begins before the point where our lips meet, when our mouths are closed, which is (in this state) the boundary.

The lips of vessels, where the concern seems to be with vessel-as-body metaphor, compared with pots made with specific utilitarian functions, is interesting. In many cases it seems to me that the lips in the former are minimal with many different makers producing a similar expression. These tend to be either a section that is a tight, rounded curve without bias to inside or outside, or a flat cut top, suggesting the end of both internal and external surfaces rather than a transition between them. This is often in association with very thin walls so that the internal shape is virtually the same as the external. The effect is to reduce the physicality of the body, perhaps suggesting the fragility of self. The intention does not seem to be with the internal volume but with the external display of internal feelings.

The choice of surface is also informative. Almost always visually attractive, rarely using glaze to clothe the pot or delineate form. Often glaze is completely rejected in favour of nurturing the surface through burnishing or staining the body with oxides.

I don't wish to disparage all such work, but it does seem to have become a clichéd response when the work's prime function is to express this idea – a familiar illustration, rather than an exploration, of identity. Perhaps we need to research more into what science can tell us, to examine this interior/exterior relationship in terms of race, gender etc.; borrow the specificity that enriches utilitarian ware and produces such a diversity of form; unzip ourselves and shine a little light on our unique physical and emotional interior.

Best wishes
Sebastian Blackie

Rim of bowl (detail)

To: Bernard Leach <bleach@ceramicheaven.com>
From: Sebastian Blackie <black@restlessearth.co.uk>

Subject: *Weight and See*

Dear Mr Leach

I remember in the 1960s, photographs of pots looked as if they had been taken by security cameras. The advantage of this was the work had little presence as an image, in fact it represented physical absence. Today, I believe, the quality and volume of photographs have reduced our understanding of ceramics. The prioritising of sight over other senses has been further reinforced by the ascendancy of clay sculpture, which generally lacks the implicit tactile engagement of pots.

The two-dimensional representation of what is significantly a multi-sensual and, usually, three-dimensional medium is problematic. If we have experienced the real thing we carry knowledge that will help us interpret other sensual experiences through the visual, but without the confirmation that handling provides, our judgements are neither informed nor refined. We can engage more physically with clay in museums and galleries but their protocols are a severe restriction. I think we need to address this in our writing.

Weight, for instance, is something little discussed but it is a quality that has values (and therefore meanings) attached to it. Generally speaking, lightness in ceramics has status. This is probably due to several factors – clay is a common material, so unlike gold, more does not increase value. Lightness in utilitarian vessels is generally desirable, as they may also have to carry a load. Lightness may also be an indicator of skill; the maker has applied judgement, the work has been weighed. Lightness, in another sense, in porcelain is a function of thinness. Here the complexity of weight begins to emerge, for thinness can also be seen as meanness. It is therefore not just dead weight but distribution of weight which is significant. This in turn relates to how the object is addressed, held, used. The tea cup is lighter than the tea bowl for many social/historical reasons but the thickness (and therefore weight) of each is related to the ergonomics of holding a hot liquid. Why then should one culture choose to embrace the vessel with both hands, which are gently warmed through the insulating thickness of the bowl's wall, while another precariously pinches a handle with one hand while the other gives additional support with a saucer? The introduction to Europe of tea and porcelain, which is an excellent conductor of heat, is closely associated and clearly significant to these two design solutions. The Spartan environment of Japanese tea rooms compared to coal-fired European drawing rooms may have also contributed, however I believe there is another element – the sexuality of weight.

Weight denotes the presence of another physical object like ourselves. The weight of a warm tea bowl may arouse memories of cupping the head or breast; we embrace each other with the same open hand.

There is so much more I could write, but perhaps it is enough to suggest a discourse. I must wait and see.

Best wishes
Sebastian Blackie

18th century porcelain teapot, New Hall, Staffordshire

To: Bernard Leach <bleach@ceramicheaven.com>
From: Sebastian Blackie <black@restlessearth.co.uk>

Subject: *Yalc!*

Dear Mr Leach

Work fired in newspaper and cardboard kilns may be subject to sudden fluctuations of temperature which, as you know, can led to dunting (cracking) through rapid and uneven expansion or shrinkage as well as steam blowing due to moisture remaining in the clay. The preheating of work by the African potters and then firing before the work cools and reabsorbs ambient moisture reduces this risk but work made with a body, which is low in plastic clay, is more likely to survive.

Years ago I made many clay body tests with Michael O'Brien who had worked with Cardew in Africa. He has a deep knowledge of ceramic technology and through him I gained some understanding of the characteristics that make for a good clay body. The first surprise was how little clay a good body contained. We tested a body, which we all agreed had excellent working properties, to discover that only 50% was clay the other half mostly comprising of extremely fine sand. We also found that bodies with a range of particle sizes generally gave good results. As a result, we designed many bodies which combined secondary clays like earthenware and ball clay, finely ground and graded in the process of their formation, with course-grained primary clays like kaolin which is found where it is formed from decomposing feldspar. We tested many sands to discover that they also showed great variation in grain size. One of my favourite bodies was made of the following in ascending order of particle size: Red Etruria Marl, AT ballclay, china clay, potash feldspar, a fine sand and soft body grog.

As you know, grog or chamotte is body filler made from ground fired clay which reduces shrinkage. Commercially available grogs tend to be fired to high temperatures. This means that they do not shrink with the other ingredients in the firing, producing a gritty surface. Soft body grog is made by

Digging mountain clay in Japan

firing a batch of your clay body to about 500°C (932°F) or lower. The low-firing temperature makes crushing by hand relatively easy before adding the grog to a second batch of clay. This grog is highly compatible as it is made from the same materials as the plastic clay and I have found it can make up a much higher proportion of the body recipe, without losing good working properties, than high temperature grog. Soft grog is particularly good for work that is burnished as it crushes easily and does not produce a speckle.

It should be no surprise that the Africans seemed to have got all this sorted long ago. I have seen a film (*Seni's Children*) of a Senegal woman making grog on an open fire in preparation for making large clay sculptures. Nevertheless, I believe it is important to interrogate the technology of others, to translate rather than mimic their methods. Techniques that work in the Sahara may not in the dampness of Britain. It is interesting that the danger of steam blowing can be reduced by firing with damp fuel producing a level of humidity around the work similar to that inside. Recently I fired clay bombs in a cardboard kiln. Bowls, designed to explode, made from fine red clay, joined rim to rim and sealed; although fired when only half-dry, some remained intact. I can only think that this was because during the packing it poured with rain and the card became quite sodden.

Doing the opposite can sometimes teach us more.

Best wishes
Sebastian Blackie

To: Bernard Leach <bleach@ceramicheaven.com>
From: Sebastian Blackie <black@restlessearth.co.uk>

Subject: *Atoms*

Dear Mr Leach

The thing I find fascinating about throwing is that it is displacing matter. Most making is either reductive, as in carving, or constructive, as in welding. Displacement means you end up with the same amount of material as you started with but in a different form. Although casting involves displacement, it requires the material to go through a liquid phase; with throwing the material remains in the same state throughout. If you combine this with the fact that there is no intervening tool between hand and material it is unique – well, almost! I have adapted the method used to pull handles to make pots. Instead of the clay revolving on a wheel I walk round the clay backwards pulling it between thumb and forefinger. Perhaps I should call it 'walking' to distinguish it from 'throwing'. It gives the same expression of plasticity as throwing but is far more tolerant of the unprocessed clay I use, with its stones and iron nodules, which makes each piece utterly individual.

Studio, Farnham, Surrey, UK. Project for Third World housing

84

Kneading clay in preparation to throw

My wife Sarah and I both wish to be cremated. Sarah would like her ashes scattered at sea; I on a stream or river. Death is an example of displacement. The atoms which currently cling together to make me have belonged to many other things in the past and will be free in the future (apart from the bits that have already dropped off) to form new identities. Combining with the atoms of other humans, known or unknown or creatures, plants, minerals etc. to make anything.

The act of throwing is interesting in that it combines a sense of individuality, separateness, with a sense of being part of everything. The clay is dug, then prepared aligning the microscopic particles so that they work together; the pot's identity then emerges from this mass in the potter's hands. There is something miraculous about this; similar to birth.

Recently I have been making work combining many individual pots to form one piece. It has changed my attitude to quality. I no longer think in terms of good and bad pots but more in terms of their individual character and how this contributes to the whole. This parallels my growing interest in collaboration and the feeling that we can achieve more together than is possible alone. I am not necessarily thinking of artists practically collaborating but opening my ideas to others. I now explain what I am doing to anyone who asks; the illiterate man who is painting our house no less than colleagues at the art school.

'Walking' the clay involves a kind of ritualistic journey. The pot is almost danced into being. The physical result is what Joanna, one of my students, has coined as 'after nature'– something

'Walking' the clay

beyond memory. Thinking about my work in this way has been greatly simulated by my MA students with their diverse backgrounds in the arts. By sticking with clay I feel I can use my hard won skills and specialist knowledge but explore ideas beyond conventional ceramic practice. A kind of displacement where the atoms of human knowledge can collaborate to form infinite possibilities.

Best wishes
Sebastian Blackie

Lifting finished pot

To: Bernard Leach <bleach@ceramicheaven.com>
From: Sebastian Blackie <black@restlessearth.co.uk>

Subject: *Humanity and Inhumanity*

Dear Mr Leach

We arrived in Hiroshima at 9am having left Kamiyahagi at midnight. About 15 miles from the city I noticed that the trees on the south west side of the hills were deformed and asked Shimada if this was as a result of the bomb. He said he thought it was pollution. We delivered some of Koie's work to his patron, a bright energetic man called Mr Satoh who has over 600 of Koie's pieces and then went on to the hotel that Mr Satoh had paid for. People's generosity in Japan is overwhelming. We had lunch on the 25th floor from which one could see the whole city. It is surrounded by mountains; a sort of bowl. I had been nervous for days about this visit and it was strange, as we ate, to think that every building I could see was my age or less. In Europe much of the military killing was almost personal: a bomb hit one house in a street leaving the others intact. Facing Hiroshima's physical presence somehow did not alleviate the dimensionless threat of the nuclear age I had grown up in.

In the afternoon we visited the Peace Museum; a mixture of crude propaganda and bizarre but eloquent artefacts. I felt guilty to recognise the beauty bestowed on mundane domestic objects by the heat of the bomb: distorted saké bottles, wonderfully deformed and 'glazed'

Bandaged and propped trees, Hiroshima Peace Park, with dome in background

masonry and the most extraordinary photograph I have ever seen – the shadow of a woman exposed on some stone steps of a bank.

She achieved a kind of immortality at the instant of her death in a medium more permanent than paper and silver nitrate. We emerged dazed and angry into the sun and wandered through the Peace Park to the famous dome, the trees were supported by props and bandaged against the frost; an image which seemed more telling than the self-conscious sculptures which litter the park. Later we went to an exhibition of tea ceremony wares. Exquisite, silent and so expressive of the materials they were made from. Both the bomb and these wares are awesome examples of man's genius; the failure of the former was a failure of imagination not creativity. I think that is why what we do as artists is so important.

On the way back to Kamiyahagi we visited a museum in Nara. I found a tiny Jomon pot, so old it is difficult to comprehend the time span it represents. No bigger than a chicken egg, formed by little more than pressing the thumb into a lump of clay, its purpose mysterious, its use of material and skill minimal but sufficient. This ancient pot is playful, generous yet austere, almost banal in scale and ambition, its expression of clayness and fire so powerful that the maker is almost eclipsed; nevertheless I deduce the presence of another human. Through this almost insignificant object I am in touch with an unknown, long dead, individual.

One can see that Koie's work, and the work of many artists of his generation, has been deeply influenced by the atom bomb just as many in Europe were influenced by the Holocaust. I have often wondered why your work seems unchanged by these momentous events. On my return to the studio I took a book at random from Koie's library. I opened it to be confronted by a photograph of the burial pits at Belsen.

Best wishes
Sebastian Blackie

Horse chestnut buds in coiled and wire-cut
vase with layer glaze by the author

Subject: *Rules*

Dear Mr Leach

In *The Ruins of Memory*, Lawrence Langer describes a German pastor breaking the laws of the Third Reich by peering through a hole in a fence to see Jews being loaded onto a train. Impotent, he leaves with a permanently tainted vision of himself.

Birmingham City Museum wants to buy a piece from the exhibition. I want to persuade them to commission a new work.

They wanted the 'Saké, Whiskey, Schnapps Cups' installation (see pp.19 and 20), but museum protocol makes it totally impractical. Each of the 1000 cups would have to be individually wrapped!

My idea is a piece called 'Goods' based on the shape of the Japanese character for goods: two squares with a rectangle above like a stack of cases – a pictograph. I plan to make it with many small, thrown cups, tossed wet into packing boxes causing the individual cups to distort and fuse into a single mass.

The piece is both a response to the optimism of 'Saké, Whiskey, Schnapps Cups' and a melding of two experiences: my visit to Japan, which included a tour of Hiroshima's Peace Museum, and visiting the Holocaust Museum in Sydney during a three month residency in Australia. It uses the fact that many cultures ritualise drinking as an act of hospitality, friendship and commemoration. The terrible beauty bestowed by the heat of the atomic bomb on domestic artefacts is linked to the image of the tangled, half-buried bodies in Belsen; an appalling consequence of a view of people as goods.

Fused saké cups

It is ironic that 'Goods' is a result of rules. Unlike the 'Saké, Whiskey, Schnapps Cups' piece, 'Goods' offers no way out. It represents a fact rather than a possibility. It is interesting that museum rules promote voyeurism and prohibit life beyond the showcase.

Best wishes
Sebastian Blackie

P.S. They have agreed to buy the 'Goods' piece!

To: Bernard Leach <bleach@ceramicheaven.com>
From: Sebastian Blackie <black@restlessearth.co.uk>

Subject: *Silent Channel*

Dear Mr Leach

My primary school has been turned into an adult education centre. I suppose it's for those who did not learn their lesson the first time!

Outside the school is a stream, now invisible under the ring road. Even as a child it was covered except for a small, turgid section abused with broken bricks and bottles. We were told that in 'the olden days', that foreign country before we were born, they sold eels from that spot.

One day our class went on a visit to a nearby factory that produced fittings for car windows. We walked, hand in grubby hand, over the invisible stream to see a writhing river of hot, black rubber. It was many years later that I realised that 'Silent Channel', the company's name, did not refer to this mysterious stretch of water.

At Fountain Abbey in Yorkshire, the Cistercian monks built a long tunnel to conceal the beautiful river Skell. What vision informed this massive commitment of manpower? Aged 15 I explored the dank, slippery space collecting as I went the waste medieval tiles; fragmented images from a time of certainty.

Britain to date has no Holocaust memorial. Soon, as the survivors die out, the memory will be sanitised by time; erased as a mistake of history. Already, for most of us, it is something that happened before our birth; buried in the past but ominously there to be re-exposed: Rwanda, Croatia, Cambodia … I should like to make something that reflects our difficulty now of dealing with this. How we disinter painful memories or reopen old wounds.

I plan to make many more 'Saké, Whiskey, Schnapps Cups' pieces and site them in a river or pit which will give them a wonderful ambiguity (are they being covered or exposed?). They will have written on them 'remember' or 'forget' in either English, Japanese or German.

To translate I will ask Nobuo, whose father said the Allies knew the Japanese were discussing surrender with the Russians before they dropped the atom bomb, and Susanne, who told me her great aunt had worked as a guard in a concentration camp.

I anticipate that over time the 'grave' will be robbed, the cups dispersed. Thus each cup will become a token of an individual, differentiated memory. A silent channel through which some lesson may be learnt.

Best wishes
Sebastian Blackie

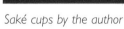

Saké cups by the author

To: Bernard Leach <bleach@ceramicheaven.com>
From: Sebastian Blackie <black@restlessearth.co.uk>

Subject: *Translation*

Dear Mr Leach

Nobuo has written to give me the Japanese characters for 'Remember' and 'Forget'. As with German, the translation is not straightforward and has to be 'do not forget' and 'forget'. He also suggests 'oblivion', made up of two characters 'loss' and 'mind' which is a good possibility as it has a secondary meaning of 'an amnesty or pardon'. He added that I write 'Blackie' with the third character smaller, otherwise it reads *butatsukii* – 'to roam about aimlessly' – very appropriate!

This weekend I was in your beloved Cornwall building kilns with Yasuo Terada. There were some very interesting similarities and differences in approach between us. My kilns follow the European tradition of updraft, the card kiln being a classic bottle kiln. Yasuo's was cross draft and similar to an Anagama. In both cases the fuel is also the kilns' structure, Yasuo uses straw bales, and both of us control the air with an outer skin of paper and slip; the Japanese kiln only being a few layers. Unlike me, Yasuo continues to nurture the kiln, modifying the intake of air and repairing ruptures in the 'skin' by covering it with wet newspaper during the firing.

Driving home I realised there are other differences. Yasuo's kiln takes its form from the material with very little modification, whereas I laboriously roll the paper or cut card. Because the paper and cardboard kilns' structures are so stable, it means little work during firing but a lot of tedious preparation.

I am thinking of designs, which gain from both strategies. One source of cardboard is the bales of flattened boxes produced by supermarkets on a daily basis. I think one could make a tunnel kiln by arranging these in two parallel rows with a third row bridging the gap to form a chamber. This would be quick to construct and provide a massive amount of fuel, a key factor in the

Cardboard kiln firing

kiln's ultimate temperature. Perhaps better still, the two rows of card bales could be pushed against an arch former to give a corbel arch with additional card added to the roof so that the external wall also takes on an arch shape. This would mean that the paper/slip outer skin would be more structurally stable and less likely to rupture as the supporting fuel shrinks as it burns.

Although my card kiln worked well, it will need a much greater volume of card to reach stoneware. I suspect that there is a limit to the size of a bottle kiln made from slip and paper and think the Anagama may be a better solution. I imagine a very elegant shape could be made with panels of card to form a curving 'whale back' kiln which is then stuffed with cut card and pots along its length. If the floor is laid with cardboard tubes it would be possible to distribute the oxygen to assist burning.

Potters experience the world uniquely. Through our work we know that clay from one place is distinctive with its own particular characteristics and that fuel from one source burns differently from another. Yasuo said that rice straw burns slower than wheat straw. The language of materials requires translation.

Best wishes
Sebastian Blackie

Cardboard kiln being built, Appledore, UK

To: Bernard Leach <bleach@ceramicheaven.com>
From: Sebastian Blackie <black@restlessearth.co.uk>

Subject: **The Garden of Eden**

Dear Mr Leach

I visited the Eden Project on the way to 'Ceramica'. Giant greenhouses (the largest in the world) have been built in a disused china clay quarry in Cornwall to house thousands of plant species. They have made a very real attempt to develop a sustainable agenda, however, it is such a success that the roads are blocked with polluting traffic. 'Eden' is not paradise. There is a sense that this second Eden embraces knowledge and we face a choice whether we treat our environment well or badly. Understanding that sustainability is complex and is as much to do with the human spirit which, if nurtured without the heavy hand of Puritanism, may reduce our material desires. There seems to be a real, holistic approach to art, technology, science and philosophy inspiring me to put forward a project.

I have a working title of *The Potter's Field*, partly as I plan to return a small piece of ceramic back to its place of origin but also because it is an extension of the biblical reference of Eden. Judas' guilt money was used to buy the potter's field to bury the dead (presumably because it was useless for anything else after the potters had finished with it). The second potter's field, like the new Eden, is a question and a challenge. The majority of china clay has been used in paper production rather than ceramics – there is then a certain irony in using paper to fire the work.

In Western society today there is a real problem in articulating the spiritual through art. Religion has appropriated the language of spirituality for so long that others assume you subscribe to a particular ideology if you make reference to it. I believe it is important to repossess the language. I am unclear how, but perhaps we could look at feminism, for example, as a model of empowerment.

The state we are in is exemplified by the Eden Project, who have adopted a Christian/Judaic language, although British society is perhaps one of the most multi-cultural in the world.

Best wishes
Sebastian Blackie

P.S. I heard today they have turned down my proposal.

Gravestone and tree, graveyard,
County Limerick, Ireland

To: Bernard Leach <bleach@ceramicheaven.com>

From: Sebastian Blackie <black@restlessearth.co.uk>

Subject: *Kiss*

Dear Mr Leach

I have often felt an empathy with doubting Thomas. For me touch is about fidelity. But Thomas gets a bad press in the Bible.

Have you seen Giotto's painting of the betrayal? It is difficult to read the painting other than as an illustration of a familiar story; the relationships known, fixed. But the image is ambiguous. As I look, I think: who betrayed whom in the garden of Gethsemane? If we have insight into one another's weakness, and knowingly exploit it, are we not, at least partly, responsible for the wrong they do through manipulation? The Giotto image does what the visual arts are so good at: it gives space for interpretation. The story is enriched by the art. The action half-concealed by curtain-like cloaks. The kiss of betrayal following the shared cup of the last supper is not a simple narrative of good and bad, but rather reveals complex relationships that have contemporary resonance. It is layered rather than linear.

I must confess to reading a page of your diary. It describes your visit to the tea master Morikawa when he offered you the ritual of Koi Cha, known as 'kiss', where the tea bowl is passed from lip to lip. Both stories indicate the symbolic potential of the vessel but neither reveals the complexity of the vessel as a mediating artefact. Not just seen but held. Touched by hand and lip.

Touch is the sense in which we are least able to disguise our real feelings. Perhaps this is why sexual betrayal is so painful. We use the same word 'feel' for literally touching another as well as our non-physical conception of another. We speak of being 'touched' when our emotions are affected by another. 'Touched' is also used to describe harmless madness or eccentricity!

Japanese tea bowls are eccentric. Although made on a wheel, which tends to produce symmetrical forms, they are asymmetrical, revealing not just the potter's touch but his energy and spirit. Using these pots is like physically experiencing another.

My first pottery teacher was a gentle giant called Louis Jones. As I struggled with the wheel he stood behind me placing his huge hands on mine and centred the clay. This simple act did not prescribe how to throw but allowed me to feel what throwing felt like; the necessary pressure, the sense of the clay running true, an insight into what I was striving for.

Today, child abuse has made teaching in this physically intimate way impossible. It is good that as a society we can think the unthinkable and struggle to protect the vulnerable. But we should not allow abusers to hijack any aspect of who we are. We need to learn through touch.

I think only two people know the true nature of what happened that night in the Biblical garden. For the rest of us, no doubt, it is a story that will be touched by our own experience of fidelity and betrayal.

Best wishes
Sebastian Blackie

'The Betrayal of Christ',
(c.1305), by Giotto,
fresco, in Srovegni (Arena)
Chapel, Padua, Italy

To: Bernard Leach <bleach@ceramicheaven.com>
From: Sebastian Blackie <black@restlessearth.co.uk>

Subject: *Banali*

Dear Mr Leach

Our flight took us over the Gobi. I could see a river, which seemed to have changed its course many times leaving tracks like hundreds of veins that disappeared into the desert. It looked as if it never reached the sea. I saw the end of the great wall trailing off into the sand (what else could it have been?), I began to see fields (I think) – huge rectangles of land with almost the same appearance as the desert. Gradually they became smaller and more intensely coloured as we approached the fertile land around Beijing. The world still has so much space without us in it. Against the insistent roar of the jet engines I imagined the silence.

In Korea I spent the five days of the festival rolling newspaper to make a kiln in which I blew up most of the work which was made only minutes before the firing. I am excited at the idea of travelling the world rendering clay objects to dust.

We were taken to the ceramic biennial at Ichon. The commitment and investment in contemporary ceramics is impressive and unthinkable in the West; but I found it deeply depressing. So much work shouting for attention and this is the homeland of your unknown craftsman! Amongst all the noise of empty vessels there was interesting stuff, but it seemed to me, that as an exhibition, it quite clearly demonstrated why ceramics is not generally accepted as a serious art form. In medieval Europe ceramics was one of the few crafts to be banished outside the city wall. I think in contemporary practice there are two tendencies which might have originated in this historical exclusion. The first is represented by the biennial; ceramic artists metaphorically knocking on the city gate. The other accepts the outcaste status. It can be anarchic, independent, subversive and sometimes fresh and interesting.

In Denmark I met Neil Forrest who teaches in Canada on Prince Edward Island (where *Anne of Green Gables* was set – Anne was the misfit orphan whose independent will eventually triumphs over the dysfunctional). He gave a really interesting presentation on Islamic ornament, which, in the true North American tradition, led us to contemporary imperatives. His work appears like a huge scientific model of some mutant bifurcating structure. It has the obsession and the assumed authority of science fiction. It is both a fiction and authentic; earth suspended in space. What I value in the work I saw Neil make is the concern with content, articulated with ceramic language. Complex yet playfully handled. He recognises the anachronism of making sculpture in ceramic in the 21st century. It reminds me of the river in the desert: sometimes there, sometimes not; constantly looking for a new way forward, perhaps never arriving, but driven on by what lies behind.

Best wishes
Sebastian Blackie

P.S. I asked Sarah how to spell lies (as in lies behind) so I did not spell it to suggest lies (untruth) behind. She told me it is spelt the same. I think that is quite banal.

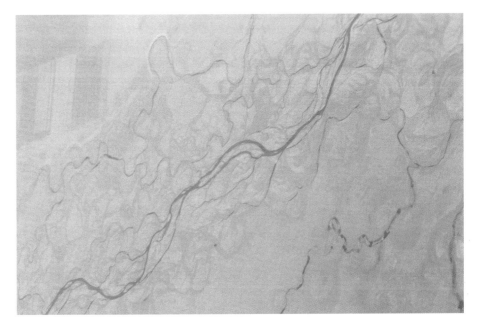

Arial view of river, Gobi desert

To: Bernard Leach <bleach@ceramicheaven.com>
From: Sebastian Blackie <black@restlessearth.co.uk>

Subject: *Big Idea*

Dear Mr Leach

I have been re-reading the transcript of the 1952 world craft conference you organised. If I understand your thesis correctly, what you are saying is that truth to material equates to truth to self which is a manifestation of a greater universal truth. That the making and, by extension, use of handcraft work makes us morally better people. Although I am living proof that this idea might be flawed, it is an idea that must have been particularly appealing after the mechanised killing of ordinary people by ordinary people in World War II. Your idea was highly influential in establishing ceramics in schools and colleges as well as a growth of interest world-wide.

For quite different reasons Josiah Wedgwood was also responsible for a sudden growth in interest. His pots result from rationalism. Form, decoration and the refined, 'unnatural' clay bodies all express domination over nature by man's intellect. Each, in your almost opposite ways, championed ceramics for what it

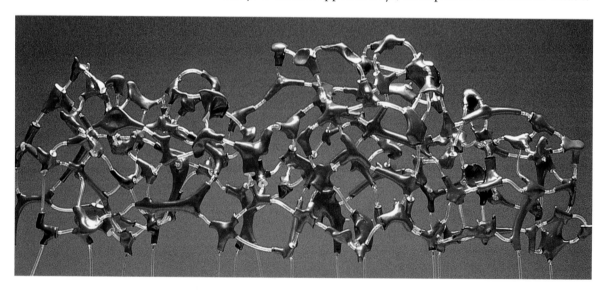

can uniquely be as well as appeal to our desire to believe in our finer qualities. There have been times in history when clay's capacity to mimic other materials has been exploited. These artefacts reveal the manipulative skill of the maker rather than their originality; they seek status by association but actually achieve the opposite.

In the UK, white has become the new brown in tableware, and sculptural practice dominates the medium. Critical analysis, what little there is, regularly compares ceramics with high-status fine art practice. This suggests mimicry and a desire for acceptance rather than a big idea.

I believe both you and Wedgwood (and others like Furuta Oribe in Japan) addressed the spiritual needs of your time. You were not for clay *per se* but used clay to reveal an idea; an idea that went beyond individual passion and found currency beyond the world of the maker.

Best wishes
Sebastian Blackie

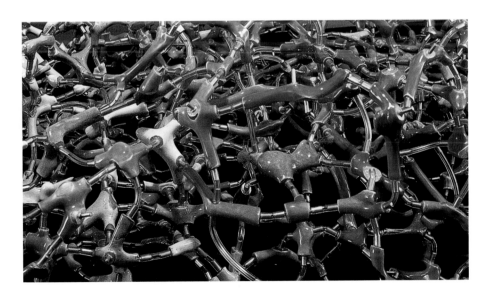

LEFT: *Work by Neil Forest*
RIGHT: *Detail*

To: Bernard Leach <bleach@ceramicheaven.com>
From: Sebastian Blackie <black@restlessearth.co.uk>

Subject *Joining Hands*

Dear Mr Leach

Today I got a message from Stan who lives out in the country, 20km from Dunedin in New Zealand. He is a deeply committed environmentalist and part-time potter. He told me he dug up what he thinks may be a Hans Coper in his garden. Extraordinary. He contacted the previous owner who told him his mother had sent it from Amsterdam, together with four live orchids. He told Stan the pot belonged with the garden and refused to take it back. The story is so rich it makes me tremble.

I cannot think of anyone who did more than you to try to form an international ceramic community. Perhaps community is the wrong word but it is amazing how clay touches such a diverse range of people who will come together despite their otherwise radical differences. There are of course distinct focuses – making, collecting, theorising, etc. Within these there are vastly varying interests. For example, making might be divided between mass industrialised and small-scale hand production – each containing groups which may feel little in common such as ceramics for automotive design on the one hand and wood-fired pottery on the other.

I have misrepresented you. It was craft, not clay, that you promoted and craft with a particular ideology. An exclusive ideology offering a greater sense of clarity than we have today but which few now can believe in. Even then not everyone agreed. I remember reading that Hans Coper felt isolated and depressed at your 1952 international conference of craftsmen (how did the women feel?).

At first sight, contemporary ceramics, which has loosely evolved from the Arts and Crafts Movement, seems to be an eclectic array of methods and concerns. Although this has broadened the boundaries, there are still vast areas of ceramic practice which are excluded. Rather arrogantly, the term 'intelligent making' has been adopted to provide some kind of definition. This I assume predicates work by intention and context. Interesting as this is, it seems to me it is just another way of controlling a hierarchy of value to the benefit of some and the rejection of others.

Years ago I was much inspired by Jean Vanier who believed the mentally handicapped (an acceptable term at the time) make a unique gift to society. Lacking the ability to project anything other than who they are, they show us humanity in a pure form. It is an inclusive philosophy, which recognises that we all have something to contribute, without precluding the exceptional. I am therefore drawn to generic definitions. An Internet of ceramics that allows individual links to be made, facilitating new relationships which may take the medium into yet unforeseen directions. We are, perhaps, too quick for our own good, to come to judgement.

At one level it does not matter whether Stan's pot turns out to be a genuine Coper; more important is whether it's a genuine pot. When I met Stan he was making ceramic fish. There was no artistic intention, yet his love and understanding of his subject, his biologist knowledge and eye gave these unpretentious pieces of clay a particular quality. We each have unique heads, hearts and hands.

Best wishes
Sebastian Blackie

Hans Coper spade form in the author's possession

To: Bernard Leach <bleach@ceramicheaven.com>
From: Sebastian Blackie <black@restlessearth.co.uk>

Subject: *Remember*

Dear Mr Leach

Shortly after Lucie Rie died I visited the college in Vienna where she had begun her career with clay. The ceramic department was in the process of being reformed as a design area. Basic physical skills marginalised in favour of paper concepts. The remaining ceramic lecturer was clearly isolated by a new ideology. Any trace of a connection with the city, mutually rejected, seems to have disappeared except perhaps with the desolate open wound of a memorial to the Holocaust placed at its centre. But the imperative of such public work appears unable to embrace the individual stories on which they are founded.

Lucie's work, for me, supremely triumphs over both memorial and its causes. It is about life – a unique, triumphant, life formed from an inner need to create rather than driven by reaction to the external forces of mass destruction. For me, her pots assert freedom. They take it as distinct from expressing it. They reveal a paradox possessing both fragility and strength – an enduring gift.

Visiting Lucie's studio in London as a student was memorable. I saw Hans Coper's work in use for the first time (another refugee from the Nazis). His spade forms full of daffodils, the 'shaft' holding the stems in a reservoir of water, the oval body spreading the blooms in

Albertinaplatz, Vienna

line with the shelf on which they stood. Until then I had seen his work as a sculptural vessel rather than a contemporary, thoughtfully designed, vase – perhaps in time his work will be considered too valuable to use and will revert to my original perception. Lucie told me that one of Hans' pots was based on one of yours but that you never realised.

On the last occasion we spoke I told her I felt I was only just beginning to understand clay. She replied, 'I feel exactly the same'. Seven years on from her death I think my comment was premature.

Ceramic is an enduring, if sometimes fragmented, medium. It outlives memory and the context in which it was made, yet can still reveal the humanity of its maker. Should this make any difference to what we do with it? It seems to me, when many artists are making stimulating work using the ephemeral, we should be thinking about this aspect of ceramics. Not particularly for moral reasons, although it is a consideration, but because it is an interesting and particular characteristic.

Best wishes
Sebastian Blackie

'Street scrubbing Jew',
Albertinaplatz,
Vienna

To: Bernard Leach <bleach@ceramicheaven.com>
From: Sebastian Blackie <black@restlessearth.co.uk>

Subject: *Bill*

Dear Mr Leach

Bill Ismay was extraordinary. Did you ever visit his home in Yorkshire? The dingy brick Victorian terrace, its curtains permanently drawn against inquisitive eyes, gave no clue to its contents. Nor the hall, just an accumulation of shabby raincoats and bérets, Bill's distinctive and unvarying attire. But to enter the kitchen was staggering. Dimly lit by a single, bare light were hundreds, perhaps thousands, of pots. Shelves lining the walls carried the detailed post-war history of British studio ceramics. The famous next to the forgotten. A lone table was covered in a multitude of ceramic boxes save for a small corner where Bill wrote and ate. The floor was a brown sea of pots with narrow causeways to allow passage to the doors and stone sink; on the draining board a tiny stove where Bill prepared coffee. He clearly delighted in testing his guests through their choice of drinking vessel, which would receive a perfunctory wipe with a rancid rag before being returned to its place marked in the dust.

Each room was overwhelming, almost impenetrable, yet somehow Bill always seemed able to reach any piece under discussion – balancing, like a dancer, his stocky frame with unexpected agility. I remember returning exhausted to the kitchen thinking our tour was complete only to be introduced to the cellar. His bedroom, strictly off limits in life, was crammed with books, photographs and letters including a protracted correspondence with a stripper, with whom he fell in love in the 1950s, which ended abruptly when she confessed she was married.

Margaret O'Rorke and Bill Ismay, Somerset, UK

Bill often ventured out to add to the collection. He travelled mostly by train and had an encyclopaedic knowledge of the rail

Bill Ismay watching a paper kiln workshop, Somerset, UK

system. In the 1960s he always seemed to be at the opening (and first in line) of every ceramic exhibition. It was rumoured that he would sleep on station platforms in order to be able to afford a purchase. Certainly his home, with its outside lavatory and peeling paint, showed no evidence that he spent any of his modest income as a librarian (and subsequently his pension) on anything other than the collection.

Is there any point in trying to analyse Bill? Perhaps, but for those of us who knew him, it would feel not only sterile, but also a violation of our relationship. I enjoyed the company of this intensely shy, passionate, incisive man. His obsession was balanced by a wry Yorkshire wit in which human endeavour is both deeply serious and simultaneously absurd. What I value most was Bill's love. He spoke of the individual pots like a proud father and of the collection as a whole as if he had created a family.

The legacy of his collection, which must now stand independently of its context, gives us a broad landscape of ceramic practice, full of glory and imperfection, to judge for ourselves. It is an alternative to the choreographed portrait, the official history, which so quickly solidifies as fact. A true gift.

Best wishes
Sebastian Blackie

To: Bernard Leach <bleach@ceramicheaven.com>
From: Sebastian Blackie <black@restlessearth.co.uk>

Subject: *Ceramic Heaven*

Dear Mr Leach

I have often mentioned Koie in my messages, let me tell you a little about him.

We first met when he made an exhibition for Galerie Besson in my studio. With the support of his assistants he produced, in two weeks, enough work for three exhibitions as well as consuming 14 bottles of malt whiskey and visiting the Neolithic stone circle at Avebury (a good 90 minute drive) five times by taxi. After a short holiday in Spain he returned to fire and glaze the work; developing, apparently by instinct, a range of glazes from an ironstone outcrop behind my house called 'The devil's jump'.

Koie is a phenomenon. He is a wild, loose, high-voltage cable igniting all in his path. But equally quiet, receptive and sensitive. He has that rare capacity to both give and take energy at the same time from those around him but leaving a positive charge.

Invitation from Koie

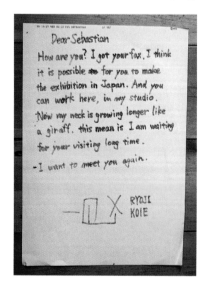

I met him again in Oxford ten years later. A year after that and I was his guest in Japan. At 6am he and his wife Sono met me from Nagoya airport. Two hours later I was in Kamiyahagi, his home and workshop deep in the foothills of the Japanese Alps. While Koie tended his garden I wandered jet lagged round the house. The cooking and eating area are on a raised platform. The table is a massive slab of American redwood that extends into the workshop to serve as a wedging bench. On one side of the workshop is Koie's fascinating library, on the other the kiln room crammed with work in various states of development and disintegration. The bamboo and pine-clad mountain rises sharply behind the house; in front the valley steeps gently down through paddy fields to the river. It had snowed that night.

RIGHT: Koie's studio with scarecrows, Kamiyahagi, Japan.
BELOW: Koie giving a riverside workshop, Kamiyahagi, Japan

During my visit the cherry blossom came and went, on my departure the fields were being planted with rice.

Koie is considered to be one of Japan's leading contemporary artists. It does not seem necessary to qualify this by adding 'ceramic' in a society where clay has such a high status. He makes pots and sculptures with equal playfulness

and vigour, apparently never losing the directness and productivity he must have acquired in his teens as a brick maker. His status has brought him wealth but he uses this with extraordinary generosity and his home has a continual flow of guests. Koie's childhood was marked by war and like many of his generation, the atomic bomb has a deep effect on his practice. He is a committed internationalist and likens himself to Hamada, and me to you, in terms of a bridge between East and West.

111

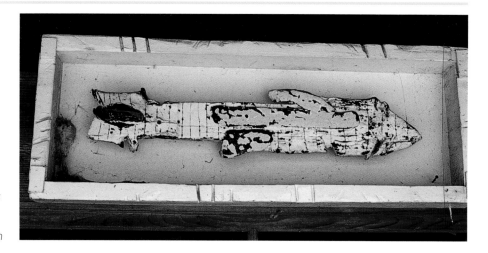

Ceramic fish over entrance to Koie's workshop, Kamiyahagi, Japan

The experience Koie gave me in Japan was so different from any other that it is more like a dream than a memory; a kind of ceramic heaven. But once discovered it is not restricted to place.

Best wishes
Sebastian Blackie

Koie killing chickens for the author's birthday, Kamiyahagi, Japan

To: Bernard Leach <bleach@ceramicheaven.com>

From: Sebastian Blackie <black@restlessearth.co.uk>

Subject: # *Death on the Nile*

Dear Mr Leach

Siddig El Nigoumi signed his work with the image of a scorpion, a tiny creature with a formidable sting.

Signing work is interesting. A stamp of ownership, responsibility, and authenticity. A simultaneous sign of both individuality and commodity.

Perhaps you know the story of Hamada, who did not sign his work. When asked how he felt about another potter who was making similar work he replied 'in a hundred years his best work will be attributed to me and my worst work will be thought to be his'. This implies an idea of authenticity that transcends authorship.

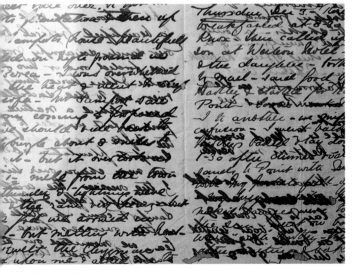

A page from my great grandfather's diary

I have a pot of yours stamped 'BL' – your finger covered the mark when you glazed the pot leaving the clay exposed, a kind of absent fingerprint around the naked clay, a tell tale half moon of thicker glaze. A clue perhaps only a potter would recognise.

I remember seeing some counterfeits of your work made by prisoners who sold them on to an auction house. They could only have fooled someone wanting to be fooled.

In many ways pots are signed all over with the maker's personality. You discuss this in *The Potter's Book*. I agree with you about the importance of

Author's fingerprint in clay

sincerity but not with your conception of the honest pot which too often seems to be a self-deluding desire for lost innocence. I find Sebastiao Salgado's images of the dispossessed stunningly beautiful and disturbing in their voyeurism – revealing something of the subject, artist and most of all, myself as viewer. I am also intrigued by the disconcerting artifice of Australian Tracey Moffat's photographs. Their representation of discordant and unsettling relationships is true to my experience of the world. I am interested in dishonest pots, subversive ceramics. A Trojan horse penetrating the domestic space, art disguised as artefact. In clay, as with most artwork, it is effective when done quietly over time like a seemingly simple question that grows in one's head.

ABOVE: *Saké cup with 'Blackie' written in Japanese characters*
ABOVE RIGHT: *Detail*

For me, Nigoumi's work has this undemonstrative sincerity. The decoration of his pots gives value to things ignored or forgotten. Weather maps, crosswords, road signs – the daily visual detritus of Western culture made attractive. These combine with the more painful memories of his Sudanese childhood, of the wonderfully decorated homes of the Nubian people drowned by the Nile after the building of the Aswan dam.

Is leaving our mark in life an attempt to trick the oblivion of death? I visited Nigoumi two days before he died; a slow alcoholic suicide. A tragic fading away. But his work lives on and is imbued with the qualities symbolised in his potter's signature. Charming, disarming, seemingly genuinely naïve yet, as if by accident, they hold a knowing sting in their tail. An honest reflection of Nigoumi's nature?

Best wishes
Sebastian Blackie

Subject: *Nest*

Dear Mr Leach

As our baby grows I experience her as a volume, with my hand on Sarah's warm belly I can feel her kick and the resistance of her head. She is a solid, sensual, sense of life.

For some months I have been looking into the void. Not the secured space of a vessel but the un-contained void of death. Finally I visited my doctor who gave me six months if I continue to smoke. It is now over three weeks since I had the last cigarette of my life, rolled by hand, the tobacco teased out, the paper deftly licked and flicked, in a ritual of making that has been as familiar in my life, but more compelling, as brushing my teeth.

What is the first thing you can remember making? In my case it is a nest built with dry hazel twigs. I remember stroking them across my lips to feel the smooth bark before carefully placing them in the fork of a tree. I do not know how old I was, two, perhaps three years-old, but looking back the obsession with the sensual quality of materials combined with the vessel has been central to my work.

Making vessels can be about exploring the space within. When I fill my lungs with air or smoke or my belly with food or alcohol, I have a sense of space; but it is contained space. The feeling of containment is reassuring. The emptiness is filled and, at the same time, the limits to emptiness are defined. The emptiness of addiction is filled (temporarily) and is experienced as a volume. Vessels, particularly clay vessels resonant with time, offer this sense of contained space in direct contrast to the limitless, terrifying void of death. But this void is fascinating, less frightening as the ability to contain weakens, and void, as void, is felt. Given up to, undefined, accepted.

I have a book on the pottery of the Mimbres people of New Mexico. I have not seen the work, but based on the photographs they seem finely made, smooth, meticulous, controlled; but dramatically almost every pot has been killed. A violent hole punctures the vessel wall destroying the calm of the mandala-like decoration (in contemporary terms the monochrome paintwork combined with the bullet-like hole has a documentary authority). It is interesting how this affects the sense of the pot's containment. One feels its spirit draining away just as a liquid would. These pots are disturbing in our time, the hole too similar to the a-aesthetic holes in the back of the excavated sculls retrieved from our many killing fields. But there is also something compelling about the clarity of these pots. They are made carefully, beautifully, in the knowledge that one day they will be destroyed. They do not subscribe to the arrogance of eternity. They have had a life.

Thinking about my nest I wonder now about its motive, and the motive for all the many vessels I have made since. Has my adult work been just an act of therapy? Did my fragile childish world of twigs seek to affirm my security or try to rebuild what I had lost? Was my nest waiting to receive life or had it already been deserted? A void-like question I think!

Best wishes
Sebastian Blackie

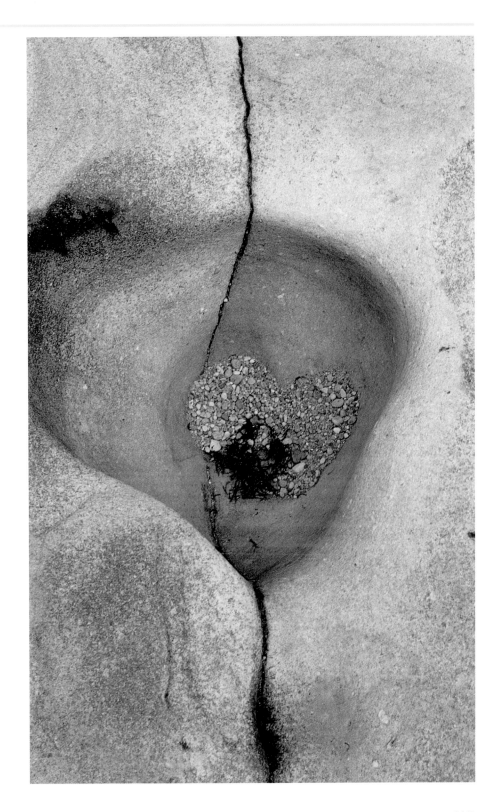

*Vessel form in
riverbed,
Wharfedale,
Yorkshire, UK*

To: Bernard Leach <bleach@ceramicheaven.com>
From: Sebastian Blackie <black@restlessearth.co.uk>

Subject: *No-thing*

Dear Mr Leach

A friend likes my messages to you but does not know where they are going. I think he may be right.

But I re-read a text by Martin Heidegger called *The Thing*. He used a jug to consider what a thing is as distinct from an object. If I have understood, he is saying the jug's 'thingness' is what it is. It is a vessel, a container of liquid, a holder of wine. The jug's appearance, its walls and base, are not however the thing. The thingness of the jug is the void, the empty nothing capable of holding wine. The thingness of the jug is also its poetic connections, the earth and sun joined to wine by vine, which the jug accepts, holds and dispenses. I think he is saying that this poetic joining brings things close even when they are distant. He points out that science tells us that the jug's void, its thingness, is not empty but full of air that the wine displaces; but in so doing reduces the jug to an object.

When we throw clay, the vessel is not trapped inside the material like Michaelangelo's slaves waiting to be released, nor are they built. We displace the solid lump of clay with an imagined sense of the void.

The thingness of pots needs to be considered in terms of time as well as space. Utilitarian pots in part relate to actions: the time it takes to wash a plate, drink a cup of coffee. But when the pot goes back on the shelf it is experienced differently. It may be ignored as an object or become a different thing because it is experienced differently.

When we fall in love it is exciting. We enjoy growing to know the other person; we become close. But in time we know them, or think we do. We may become bored and seek out another. But the best is beyond bored. Beyond is the thingness of our lover, the unknowable other. For me, Giacometti's sculptures and drawings are about this as is Hans Coper's work. As a potter and refugee without family, Coper was drawn to Giacometti because he was obsessed with trying to touch this unknowable other.

Words are more inclined to be linear but my messages are not trying to go anywhere. Like the act of throwing, they move round and up to create space. A space that may be filled with the experience of others, just as the jug is filled with wine. The words do not form a circle, which is complete, but spiral up so that ideas are lifted, squeezed and aligned. My words, I hope, are like the walls and base of the jug; intimately containing within them the empty, unknowable, void. The thing.

Best wishes
Sebastian Blackie

*Jug; coiled and slabbed, saggar-fired
stoneware by the author.
W.A. Ismay Collection, Yorkshire
Museum, UK*

To: Bernard Leach <bleach@ceramicheaven.com>
From: Sebastian Blackie <black@restlessearth.co.uk>

Subject: *Begin-again*

Dear Mr Leach

Last night the earth moved. Despite my visits to Japan and New Zealand this was my first experience of an earthquake, and in England! How odd to be excited by a force that demonstrates our insignificance. Perhaps it's the appeal of being removed from the familiar, an awesome power that shakes the mental, as well as the physical, walls with which we surround ourselves.

In your letter you said you were off on your travels again. Was it Australia and New Zealand? I am interested in your account of that trip, so perfunctory in your description of Australia but effusive of New Zealand.

I imagine you did not go down well down under. The Australians have historical reasons to dislike the English middle-class style. They are fair, but suspicious of reputations and take you as they find you. I suspect you may not have warmed to their irreverence. Ironically, despite your proselytising of the unknown craftsman, you seemed to have enjoyed the limelight. As a student I forged a ticket to attend a lecture by you and Hamada and you were clearly jealous that Hamada attracted all the attention.

During my three-month stretch I found Australia a disturbing country. The bush feels immensely old, pre-human, frighteningly beautiful, subtle and addictive. Its sprawling coastal cities could hardly be more different. My contact was almost exclusively with the new Australian '£10 poms', Greeks and Italians, and more recent immigrants from Asia and South Africa.

As a temporary visitor to the city, the Aborigines seemed almost invisible.

I found the people simultaneously familiar and alien, open and defensive, confident and insecure. The country's intense light bleaches the mid-distance,

The National Art School, Sydney (formerly Darlinghurst Jail)

producing a very different kind of perspective. Australians are optimistic and energetic but I found they had an eerie, almost hostile, disinterest in the past. My studio in Sydney was a cellblock. The art school a convict-built prison – a dubious national monument! The massive perimeter wall, known as the meat rack, where sex and drugs are traded on one side and life classes taught on the other, holds the college in its physical and psychological grip. Ambiguous in its function, the college is a graphic symbol of art's position in society and society's view of art.

You were born in China and grew up in Japan. Your sense of home must be very different to mine whose childhood was restricted to a small English village. For me, the main purpose in travel is to be changed by it, to be shaken. An exciting, but frightening prospect.

I am shortly returning to India. Exploring the subcontinent alone. I think it will be my most demanding journey yet.

I will e-mail you.

Best wishes
Sebastian Blackie

The author scaling a wall using rope made from newspaper

*'English' pot, coiled and
wire cut by the author*

Biographies

Michael Cardew was Bernard Leach's most influential pupil. An Oxford scholar, he embraced studio ceramics with zeal informed by such diverse stimulus as Greek philosophy and socialist ideology. His ideas were directly descended from Ruskin. His most public contribution was to make a bridge that gave pragmatic makers an insight into the scientific theory of ceramics. For many years he worked in Africa developing stoneware pottery using local materials. In 1959, urged on by my teacher Henry Hammond, he gave a course of lectures on geology and raw materials for the potters called *Fundamental Pottery*. This provided the basis for his book *Pioneer Pottery* published ten years later. He was a charismatic man; articulate, energetic and passionate. He took a dim view of art schools, but when I suggested they offered the opportunity to play, he replied 'Play, now that is *really* important'.

Hans Coper came to Britain, a refugee from the Nazis. As a German Jew, his suffering did not cease on arriving in the UK and he endured internment and hard physical work which damaged his health. Coper trained as an engineer but began to pot when he met Lucie Rie at the end of the war in 1945. Lucie claimed she never taught him and always considered him a better potter than herself. They initially worked together and regularly exhibited together throughout his career. Coper's work has an intensity that is difficult to resist; perhaps born of earlier hardship and the trauma of the Holocaust. The main body of his work is usable vessels but with a strong sculptural sensibility. Coper and Rie represented a very different kind of ceramics to Leach, who imported ideas from Japan that in many ways echoed and reinforced the existing bucolic values of the English middle class. While Leach preached, Coper questioned – most famously he would ask 'why not how' (are you making). He belonged to a studio rather than a workshop tradition and his students at the Royal College of Art did not reflect his style in the way Leach's do. His ideas did not demand ideological conformity and he justified his choice of career on the basis that all human endeavour was absurd. Coper described himself as being like a demented piano tuner trying to find the perfect pitch; a description I am unable to improve on.

Ryoji Koie was born in 1938 in the fishing and potting town of Tokoname, Aichi Prefecture, Japan. Traditions of pot making in Tokoname can be traced back to the late Heian period (AD794-1185) and it became known as one of the six ancient kilns of Japan. His mother died when he was four and he had a bad relationship with his father, a soldier in the imperial army, perhaps establishing a life-long hatred of militarism subsequently reinforced by the atomic bombing of Japan. He left school at 14 for a pipe factory where he had worked part-time since he was 10 and continued with the demanding manual labour of the heavy clay industry throughout his teens, despite losing two fingers of his right hand. While Koie subsequently gained a knowledge of ceramic technical theory at college, the productivity and direct use of clay of this period has been characteristic of his practice thoughout his career. Koie's anarchic spirit thrived in post-war Japan, which was engaged in reappraising its past. Deeply affected by the reality of the atomic bomb, he, like most of his generation, radically questioned practice. He has a rare commitment to both his local community and internationalism and has travelled extensively overseas receiving many honours. Koie shares the spontaneity and some of the ideas of the 16th century tea master Furuta Oribe, who believed in sharing the 'Way of Tea' to all, regardless of rank. In Koie's home you may find the local woodcutter sharing the same dish (cooked by Koie) with a curator from one of America's top galleries. Or an impoverished student from New Zealand discussing work with a Japanese collector who has just spent thousands on Koie's work together with an artisan from Europe, whose entire visit Koie has funded. In 1992 he was made Professor at Aichi University of Fine Arts where he is driven (under protest, and often under alcoholic influence) once a week to teach. In 2001 he was honoured with the 'Oribe' award (named after the tea master) for innovation and creativity. It is difficult for me to offer an objective view of Koie's impact, but of all the makers I have met he is the most dynamic and inspiring ambassador of contemporary ceramics.

Bernard Leach was born in Hong Kong and spent much of his childhood in Japan. After an abortive training as a banker in London, his father, a solicitor, agreed to him studying art. In 1909 he returned to Japan to teach etching where he was introduced to pottery and subsequently studied ceramics under the master Ogata Kenzan. In Japan he developed a highly influential group of friends including the potter Hamada and the philosopher Yanagi,

'Sink', coiled and pinched saggar-fired stoneware by the author

responsible for the *Mingai* (craft revival) movement. In 1920 he returned to the UK to establish a pottery in St Ives, Cornwall. Leach was the key figure in the 20th century studio ceramics movement and wrote a compelling philosophy in his publication *A Potter's Book,* which for some gained almost Biblical status. He introduced to the Western end of Eurasia an Eastern appreciation of ceramics, helping Europeans to understand more deeply the exotic imports from the Orient. He travelled and lectured extensively, championing the value of craft practice.

Siddig El Nigoumi initially trained as a calligrapher in the Sudan where he won a scholarship to study ceramics at the Central School of Art, London. While studying in England he met his wife Vicky, a textile designer, and they returned to Africa where Nigoumi taught at the National Art School in Khartoum until resigning from his post due to a dispute over policy between the college staff and government. He brought his young family back to Britain in the mid 60s, working first as a technician and later as a teacher at Farnham School of Art (subsequently known as the Surrey Institute). The ceramic department at that time was led by Henry Hammond who combined the workshop traditions of Michael Cardew with the artistic concerns of William Staite-Murray (Henry's ceramic teacher at the Royal College of Art). At this time Nigoumi's work reflected his excitement in the visual stimulus of a new country as well as his fresh memories of the culture he had left behind.

His forms were coiled or pressed but he decorated with high-temperature glazes unknown in the African tradition. Nigoumi, as he was known to his family and friends, exhibited widely and was invited to tour New Zealand by their Ceramic Society (having been imprisoned on the way for eight hours in case he tried to enter the USA illegally). Nigoumi was unassuming, with impeccable, natural good manners but seemed to lack the skills to capitalise on his success. His work was not traditionally African but a poetic product of living in Europe as well as the African and Arab cultures that are fused in the Sudan. In Magdalene Odondu's view he was the most successful of his generation of ex-patriot Africans at synthesising British and African cultures. But his worked lacked overt 'knowingness' and was apparently too naïve and rustic to be fully accepted by the UK craft establishment of the 1970s, who were trying to distance themselves from the rural image of craft and develop an agenda using contemporary fine art theory. Somehow Nigoumi got lost between two worlds. As his family grew and dispersed, his work became more subdued; the decorative subject matter, scratched on dry unglazed clay, dependent on childhood memories of the arid region of Kordofan in western Sudan. In the last years of his life he spent more time drinking than making, and eventually died of liver failure in 1995.

Furuta Oribe was a Japanese warrior and tea master of the Momoyama period at the turn of the 16th and 17th century, a time of relative peace but social and economic upheaval. During this period Japan had opened up to foreign trade and influence, a new ruling class had emerged which was less referential to traditional courtly protocols and although quickly fetishised by Japanese rituals, open to new influences. The style of work known as Oribe is thought to have been introduced to Japan by Marco Polo or alternatively to have come from Persia via Vietnam. Its development in Japan as stoneware was, in part, due to the improved technology of the Noborigama (multi-chambered) kiln. The foremost tea master of his day, Furuta Oribe, known for his innovative approach to the tea ceremony, became patron to this flamboyant and eclectic ware which, as a result, became widely popular. Oribe ware is playful and extremely diverse. It was made in such quantity that it would have been impossible for one man to have overall control; thus one may assume that Furuta Oribe inspired the work or created a sympathetic environment in which the potters could experiment. Oribe was the chosen successor of Rikyu, regarded as the greatest tea master of all time. Rikyu

Stacking tea bowl vase, thrown and assembled saggar-fired stoneware by the author

established a 'way of tea' that profoundly influences Japanese aesthetics and philosophy to this day. He formulated the Zen-inspired concept of *wabi* and *sabi*, for which there are no Western equivalents, but which inform the Japanese taste for minimalism and use of natural materials. Both men displayed an extreme capacity for combining discipline and anarchic spontaneity, which over 400 years later I, for one, find breathtaking.

Lucie Rie was born into the wealthy, cultured, Jewish, community of 1902 Vienna. She studied ceramics at the Kunstgewerbeschule and won several international prizes for her work before emigrating to England, where her work was unknown, to escape Nazi persecution. She quickly made friends with Bernard Leach who offered vital support despite him having little sympathy with her work. In effect, she was obliged to start her career from scratch and began by producing ceramic buttons for the fashion industry. Nevertheless, she quickly found an enthusiastic audience for her pots, particularly from other Jewish refugees. As interest in the rustic, oriental-inspired Leach aesthetic waned, the urban sophistication and elegance of Rie's work began to make an impact on British ceramics. However, it was not until she was at the age when most people retire, that Rie gained wider recognition and began to exhibit in major museums in Europe and America. There is a certain irony that one of her last major exhibitions was in Japan; attracted initially by the buttons Lucie had produced in the 1940s, the fashion designer Issey Miyake organised an exhibition of her work in Tokyo. She continued to pot into her eighties, rising at four each morning until a stroke terminated her long career.

Josiah Wedgwood was one of the great figures of Britain's Industrial Revolution, combining a methodical approach to ceramic technology with a design sense that recognised the aspirations and taste of the late 18th century. His genius for business is evident in his successful embracing of the new technologies of his time to include building a canal between Stoke-on-Trent and Manchester to enable him to export to Europe and the colonies. Although of humble origins, his ability quickly brought him success and acceptance. As a member of the Royal Society he exchanged ideas with the great scientists and thinkers of his time and was engaged in applying systematic methods to ceramic glazes and clay bodies. This enabled him to produce work that met the tastes and standards of nobility as well as an expanding middle class made wealthy by the development of industry and new farming methods. His forms were based on the pots of classical Greece made popular in the 'Age of Reason' due to the association with rational thought and scientific study. Although a successful businessman, he was driven by idealism rather than money – welcoming both the French Revolution and the independence of America despite their negative effect on his trade. He was a good employer and vehemently against slavery, producing an anti-slavery medallion which he distributed for free. Benjamin Franklin wrote to Wedgwood that he believed they 'may have an effect equal to that of the best written pamphlet'. It seems extraordinary that Wedgwood, who started business in a town which lacked even a road, should later have bought clay from both Australia and the Carolinas in the USA (from the Cherokee Indian nation) in his tireless investigation of ceramics.

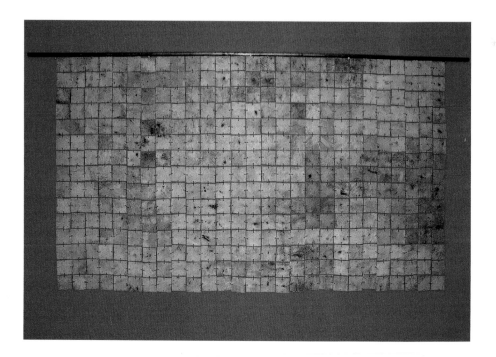

Ceramic carpet
104x183 cm
(41x72 in)